ABOUT MY FATHER'S BUSINESS

*

Lillian Beckwith was born in a Cheshire industrial town and was educated in Runcorn and Birkenhead. She later became a teacher in an infants' school and then did secretarial work for the local Henpecked Husbands Club. Eventually, however, ill health and a modicum of financial independence took her to Bruach, and it was then that her adventures began. Having served a hilarious crofting apprenticeship, described in her book THE HILLS IS LONELY, she acquired her own cottage and croft. Her experiences as a crofter she recounted in THE SEA FOR BREAKFAST and THE LOUD HALO.

The Western Highlands were also the setting for her novel GREEN HAND, which like the other books was and is highly successful.

She now lives in the Isle of Man, where, she says, easily her favourite pursuit is roaming the shore collecting driftwood. Her other activities, apart from writing, include running a boutique and writing and producing amateur pantomimes. 'I love work and always take on too much,' she says.

Also in Arrow Books by Lillian Beckwith

Lillian Beckwith

About My Father's Business

decorations by
DOUGLAS HALL

ARROW BOOKS

ARROW BOOKS LTD
3 Fitzroy Square, London W1

An imprint of the Hutchinson Publishing Group

London Melbourne Sydney Auckland
Wellington Johannesburg Cape Town
and agencies throughout the world

First published by
Hutchinson & Co (*Publishers*) Ltd 1971
Arrow edition 1973
Second impression 1974

*Made and printed in Great Britain
by The Anchor Press Ltd,
Tiptree, Essex*

ISBN 0 09 907780 9

In memory of my father

I

The tarred boards of the old pigsty had blistered in the hot sun and the blisters dried to a brittleness that was like the burned skin of the rice pudding my mother had left in the oven the whole of the previous day. Fran and I stood close against the sun-warmed boards, seeking out the largest and crispest blisters, piercing them with our thumbnails until they split with a satisfying 'pop' to reveal the splodges of raw wood, pale as straw beneath the black coating. The most promising blisters were at the top of the pigsty, just out of my reach even when I stood on my toes and stretched as hard as I could. But Fran was taller. She reached up and 'popped' them with a thumbnail that was longer than any I was ever allowed to grow. She turned her smug, puckered grin on me.

'I'm taller than you are,' she asserted.

'I know,' I admitted ruefully. Only that morning Charlie, the stable boy, had at our request measured us against the height of his new yard broom and there had been no disputing the fact that Fran's notch was two of Charlie's fat finger widths higher than mine. It was sad to be smaller than your best friend, especially when she was three days younger.

'And I can run faster and jump higher,' she pursued.

I nodded. Of course Fran could run faster and jump higher. She wasn't short and podgy like me. Head bent, I stirred the fine earth that had once been pig litter with the toe of my blancoed plimsoll.

'And I'm prettier.' Fran tossed back her drape of glinting fair hair, lifting it away from the nape of her neck with a tanned and grubby hand.

We smiled at each other in complete agreement. Too often I had heard my mother deploring my own lack of beauty; too often heard adults enthusing over Fran's prettiness and daintiness, whereas after they had assessed my plump body, my pale cheeks, brown eyes and mousy hair constrained into a thin pigtail the only compliment they could bring themselves to offer was 'What a pretty bow of ribbon you have tying your hair.' At least I had that. My huge ribbon bows were the envy of my friends and were Mother's despairing yet determined attempt to make me as attractive as other children. Each bow took three-quarters of a yard of four-inch-wide ribbon, notched into a 'V' at each end to discourage fraying, and they were always the most flamboyant colours she could find: rainbow ribbons, shot-silk ribbons, moire ribbons, double-sided satin ribbons, silk ribbons, taffeta ribbons; she sought them and bought them as persistently as I wore them and lost them. Much as I enjoyed wearing such distinctive ribbons there were times when I envied Fran her plain Alice band. Alice bands didn't slip off so easily as ribbons, nor were they so tempting to the naughty boys who crept up behind one and with a snatch and a whoop of triumph dashed away with their trophy. Fran never had to face her mother's irate questioning as to the whereabouts of her hair ribbons nor endure the subsequent reprimand; she was never made miserable by threats that next time it would be a torn piece of rag she would have to wear on her hair, like the despised bargee children.

There were many things I envied Fran. I wished my parents were as happy-go-lucky as hers; I wished I had her fair hair, blue eyes and rosy cheeks, a combination which adults, particularly schoolteachers, associated with an angelic character as obstinately as they associated plainness with badness. Sometimes when Fran had beguiled some adult into sparing her whilst meting out to me the punishment for a joint misdeed my envy flared into brief sulky resentment. Brief because Fran was an anxious commiserator on such occasions. She was genuinely sorry I was not pretty and consoled me by repeating her mother's assertion that the beautiful actresses we sometimes glimpsed on their way to the local Hippodrome hadn't been born beautiful but had made themselves so with paint and powder and hair dye. Fran was quite sure I could do the same as soon as I was old enough. She couldn't hold out any hope for my eyes though. So far as either of us knew the doctors hadn't yet managed to change 'brown eyes pick-a-pie' into 'blue eyes beauty'. But I had great faith in doctors. By the time I grew up I was confident they would be able to dye brown eyes blue.

9

Usually after Fran had indulged in a little boasting I had to do something energetic to cheer myself up but today I was full of an elation that left no room for even a trace of despondency. Today I could retaliate with something that would make me the object of envy. I took a deep breath.

'I've got a secret!' I announced.

Fran looked at me as though she expected me to be telling a story, which was our euphemism for a downright lie.

'What sort of a secret?' she demanded.

A secret with us could be anything from proclaiming the discovery that Sergeant Zagger had bought a nanny goat which he kept in Archer's field to tittering the information that the lady from the Maypole had joined the Salvation Army; from divulging that a classmate had bugs in her hair to disclosing that Charlie, the stable boy, only got black pudding for his Sunday dinner.

'This is a really truly secret,' I affirmed. A 'really truly secret' was one that made you sick with the excitement of knowing it; a secret that you'd promised, on your honour, never to tell anyone.

'Are you going to tell me?' asked Fran, leaning close.

I looked at her for a moment to ascertain whether she was in a serious enough mood to receive my prodigious news. I was pricked by the memory of my promise to Father.

'No,' I replied. 'I mustn't.'

Fran looked crestfallen. 'Is it a nice secret?' she probed.

I nodded, slowly and exaggeratedly.

'As nice as mine when I had a baby brother?'

I didn't think much of Fran's baby brother. 'Nicer,' I said.

Fran sucked in her breath. She was staring at me with wide, incredulous eyes and I began to think she was at last solemn enough to be told the secret I was longing to reveal. Still I held back.

'I'll tell you tomorrow,' I said.

'Why not today?'

'Because.'

'Because what?' She pulled at my pigtail as if it had been a bell rope.

'Because I promised not to,' I retorted, grabbing at her hand.

Fran wandered away a few steps and picked up some pebbles, tossing them from her palm on to the back of her hand. I was suddenly afraid she was losing interest.

'I ought not to, really,' I repeated.

Fran threw down the pebbles. 'If you're going to break your promise tomorrow you might just as well break it today,' she said petulantly, and seeing that I was swayed by her logic her voice became coaxing. 'Tell me now and God will choke me if I tell it to anyone else.' She spat the requisite three times and touched her throat to convince me and the Almighty of the earnestness of her pledge. I could hold out no longer.

'We're going to open a shop!' I whispered the words at the boards of the shed and then turned swiftly to face Fran so that she would know I was telling the truth.

Her expression was ecstatic. 'A shop?' Her voice was squeaky with wonder. 'A sweet shop?'

Her question was exactly the one I had asked my parents when they had first told me of the project.

'No, not a sweet shop,' I told her. 'It's to be a grocery and provision shop but we're going to sell some sweets as well.'

'What sorts?' demanded Fran.

'Only the ones my mother likes,' I said, a trifle apologetically, hoping she wasn't going to feel as cheated as I had.

There was a moment of silence and then Fran asked: 'Does your mother like Kali suckers?'

I shook my head.

'Peggy's legs or coconut kisses?' Fran was naming our current favourites.

'No.'

'Scented jujubes; liquorice comfits?'

I continued shaking my head slowly from side to side while she reeled off the names of all the sweets displayed in little sun-stickied heaps on lace d'oyleys in Mrs Lett's shop window.

Fran gave up. 'What does your mother like?' she asked.

'Paradise drops, glacier mints and peppermint lozenges.' I tried, without much success, to infuse a little rapture into my voice.

Fran pulled a face. I resorted to digging a thumbnail under each of my fingernails in turn in an attempt to prize out the embedded tar which by now had begun to sting.

'I suppose we could get to like paradise drops and glacier mints?' I suggested hopefully.

'I suppose we could if we got a lot for a penny.' Fran was quiet for a moment. 'Will you be able to weigh my sweets for me and make the scale go down with a bump?' she questioned with renewed interest.

'Oh, yes!' I breathed. The prospect of weighing out any sort of sweets made me dreamy with delight. 'I won't be like Skinny Letty.' We giggled.

Old Mrs Lett never allowed the scale to go down with a bump. Indeed it was difficult to perceive that the weight pan lifted at all when she served us. Father always laughed when we grumbled about Mrs Lett and said God must have had a little bit of humanity left over after He'd finished work and so He'd given it to one of his young angels who'd shaped it into a little Mrs Lett much in the same way as I shaped little figures out of the scraps of pastry Mother had left over on baking day. She was such a tiny wisp of a woman with a pink puckered face and scanty white hair that looked as if it had blown off a seeded dandelion. The lenses of her spectacles were as thick as the bottle-glass panes of her shop window so that you couldn't see if there were real eyes behind them and her voice was so fragmentary that when she glided out from the kitchen into the shop to stand looking at us enquiringly we were never sure whether or not she had greeted us. While she waited for us to make up our minds she constantly squeezed her spongy pink hands in the folds of the sack apron she always wore. However long we might take to choose our purchases she took at least as long to serve us. She hated parting with her sweets, dropping them one at a time into the scale, exchanging a smaller one for a bigger one if she detected the slightest tremor of the chains that held the weight pan and crouching every now and then to peer at it in case it had stuck. She was so mean she even kept a pair of scissors on the counter to cut dolly mixtures in half.

'If you're going to have a grocery shop won't you be selling cocoa and sugar and butter?' Fran asked, suddenly eager again.

'Of course!' I exclaimed happily. When there was no money for sweets it was our custom to beg from our respective parents a small square of paper in the centre of which were placed a knob of butter, a pinch of cocoa and a teaspoonful of sugar. We would gather up the corners of the paper, squeeze it gently so that the ingredients became well mixed and then lick at the resulting concoction. If we could lick the paper clean without making too much mess of ourselves it was sometimes possible to beg a second helping.

Fran croodled down, leaning back against the shed. I slid down beside her.

'Are you going to have your shop in the kitchen or in the parlour?' Fran asked, looking towards the house.

I suddenly realised that I hadn't told Fran the next most important part of my secret.

'Neither,' I replied. 'It's to be up above the railway station.'

'Above the station?' Fran was concerned. The railway station cut the town in half and 'above the station' was virtually foreign country to us. We only got that far when escorted by our parents. 'Are you going to live up there too?'

'Yes.'

'You're flitting from here?'

'Yes.'

'When?'

I wasn't quite sure when but I understood it was to be soon.

'Shan't we be able to play together here any more?'

It was gratifying to see how downcast Fran looked and I was about to reassure her that of course we should still be able to play together around the well-loved stables; the wide cobbled yard with its outside tap wrapped in sacking; the old pigsties and black sheds. But as I opened my mouth to speak it smote me suddenly that it wouldn't be true. The familiar surroundings would no longer be our sanctuary; perhaps other children—and I had no doubt they would be horrid ones—would be discovering our secret hiding places among the sheds; the dim cosiness of the hayloft; the warm embrace of hay-filled mangers. I began to feel quite tearful at the thought of leaving it all and yet it wasn't so bad for me as for Fran. I was buoyed up with the prospect of a new home and new adventures and discoveries. Fran had nothing to look forward to but the loss of her playmate and the playground which had become our safe enclosed world into which bullying boys and spiteful girls could pursue us no further than the big iron gates of the drive.

'Oh, you won't 'alf cop it when your father sees that!' I spun round guiltily as the voice of Charlie, the stable boy, assailed us. Fran was more leisurely. Charlie had a harness brush in his hand and he was pointing it accusingly at the pigsty like a schoolmaster pointing a cane. 'You've made it look proper shot at,' he gloated.

We stood back and stared horrified at our handiwork of the afternoon. Charlie was right. The shed was hideous with its pockmarks of burst blisters.

'You just wait till your father sees what you've done, that's all,' he taunted.

'Go away, patchy pants!'

Charlie blushed at Fran's gibe and backed towards the stables as she picked up a handful of gravel and threw it after him. I felt a fleeting moment of pity for Charlie, wondering if the new children to come to Wesley House would jeer at his patched pants and black-pudding dinners even more cruelly than we.

'Will you really get into a row?' Fran asked anxiously.

I found I was biting my lip with worry, but I tossed my head. 'I don't care if I do,' I said carelessly, and Fran, suspecting it was tantamount to an admission that I would and that I was already scared stiff, smoothed her dress and adjusted her Alice band.

'I'd better go home now,' she said hurriedly. 'I expect it's time for my tea.'

'But I haven't had my tea yet,' I protested. Fran's teatime was always much later than mine and the signal for her to go came when I was called. Mother refused to have friends waiting about for me while I ate. She said it made me bolt my food.

'I expect your tea's late tonight,' said Fran glibly. She pirouetted so that her skirt swirled around her thighs and showed a frilly white petticoat threaded with red ribbon round the hem. I sulked, wishing I could pirouette as gracefully as Fran and that when I tried to my dress would swirl up and show white frilly petticoats. But I couldn't pirouette and, because Mother thought wide skirts both improper and extravagant, there was never enough material in my dresses to lift and show my petticoats which, though they might be white, were never frilly nor ribbon-trimmed.

'If you're still being punished tomorrow and have to stay inside, come to the window and I'll dance for you outside the gates,' Fran offered, and seeing that I was not much cheered by the prospect she added comfortingly: 'I can make funny faces at you through the gate, too.' Fran was good at making funny faces and I slipped her a tiny smile. She went tripping away home to her indulgent parents, skirts flouncing against her legs as rhythmically as water in a swinging pail. I slunk behind the pigsty to await Father's return from work and the inevitable scolding.

.   .   .   .   .

My home at this time was Wesley House which had been built originally by Uncle Dick for his own occupation. Uncle Dick, with whom there was in reality only a distant degree of relationship, was an unlovable character. As a youth he had emigrated to America and having made there what he estimated to be sufficient fortune had returned to his native village with a view to becoming its squire. There he bought a sizable area of land and built for himself what he liked to refer to as a 'gentleman's residence' complete with stables, coach-house and ancillary buildings, all surrounded by shrubberies, gardens and extensive lawns. Having thus established himself as a passable imitation of a gentleman he then set about establishing himself as a passable imitation of a saint—an infinitely more difficult task since his reputation had earned for him locally the nickname of 'Masher Dick'. The first step towards attesting his piety was to name the new residence Wesley House. The second was to build a Wesleyan chapel just outside the drive gates, 'handy for constant worship'. These somewhat extravagant gestures undoubtedly impressed the neighbours and earned for him a show of respect from the numerous devotees of the new chapel. The rest, it must be admitted, continued to regard him as what they rightly judged him to be—a rogue on weekdays and a bigot on Sundays.

Uncle Dick was a large man in height and girth; his arms

though thick and strong as cart shafts were soft-fleshed like newly boiled ham skin; his eyes were hard and green as the glass marbles in pop bottles and except when he was addressing the congregation in his capacity of lay preacher or struggling to achieve baritone resonance as the self-appointed leader of the choir his voice was raspingly imperious. He was mean and he was money-grubbing and he missed no opportunity to profit no matter at whose expense it might be. However, in the rapidly spreading village which had known no indigenous gentry he was allowed to assume the role of a gentleman, a role which he played with great aplomb. Every day he liked to be seen riding out on a big white horse called Dolly; nodding arrogantly to passers-by and then returning at a gallop which grew more impressive as he neared the boundaries of his own demesne. Dolly would thunder up to the drive gates, her mane streaming behind her, and there Uncle Dick would rein her in and rap impatiently with his whip on the iron gates until the stable boy ran to hold them open for him. When he married it was to a woman even more socially ambitious than himself. She demanded a more imposing residence than Wesley House so he built Westminster House at the opposite end of the drive and there settled with his bride. My parents, good chapel folk who had met while they were both singing in the choir of the Wesleyan chapel, were offered Wesley House for their home and as by this time Uncle Dick had opened a grocery shop and appointed Father as manager, they were delighted to accept the offer. It was here that I was born. In the cobbled yard I took my first steps, reaped my first bruises and imbibed the smell and sounds of occupied stables. It was here that the various stages of my childhood were photographed by Father with his cherished plate camera; and here that I watched for the blooming of the purple lilac tree just outside the kitchen window. It was here too that I had brought my first playmate, Fran, to help me bury

17

with tears and ritual the baby starlings that fell from the nests in the eaves; to play hide-and-seek in the lofts above the stables and coach-house; to sail stick boats on the big horse trough and ride broomstick horses along the poplar-lined drive.

It was perverse of me to have chosen Fran for my friend. To have introduced into such a citadel of Wesleyanism the daughter of a publican. It might not have been so heinous if Fran's parents had been high-class publicans but this they were most certainly not. They kept what was easily the most sordid tavern in the town, a small whitewashed inn down by the canal frequented only by bargees, dockers and itinerants. A place where people sat outside on summer evenings and allowed themselves to be seen drinking or even dancing to the music of the barrel-organ. A place ordinary decent sinners kept away from. People said that Fran's father was never sober and that her mother was too happy, which didn't please the Wesleyans. But despite coaxing and persuasion and constant inducements to play with more suitable children Fran remained my favoured companion and because she was invariably clean and well dressed and our friendship was never marred by strife and bickerings my parents grudgingly allowed it to continue though always on the strict understanding that I must never pay a reciprocal visit to Fran's home and the equally strict undertaking to keep well out of the way of 'Aunty Rye'.

Aunty Rye was Uncle Dick's wife. Her name was Maria but her husband had shortened it to the diminutive 'Rye' and 'Rye' she became to my parents. To me she was Aunty Rye, though behind her back I spoke of her as 'Aunty-Rye-num', which Father said was the name of a flower that dragon's spat out because they didn't like the taste of it. She was a most awesome woman, tall and string thin, and always it seemed to me, attired for visiting or chapel in high-waisted dresses that fell in folds round thin, button-booted ankles; she regularly wore a fur tippet and carried a parasol in one hand and a reticule in the other, the whole being topped by a hat like an open fruit pie, pierced with hat pins and swathed in veiling. I cannot recall her face, it was so infrequently unveiled. She did not like children at any time and when she condescended to speak to me it was usually to ask if I had been to Sunday school or whether I remembered to say my prayers regularly. Her eyes regarding me through the veiling looked as yellow and spiteful as those of Aunty Pugh's poll parrot which used to glare at me through the bars of its cage. Once when I had put my face too close to the cage the parrot had pecked my nose. I was always careful not to put my face too close to Aunty Rye. I think it was on my fourth birthday and soon after I had recovered from a bout of chicken-pox that Aunty Rye, who must have been feeling in a Lady Bountiful mood, came to visit me, bringing with her a beautifully dressed doll. The doll was for me, she said, but only if I could recite for her my nightly prayer without faltering. Eager to earn the gift I knelt down, closed my eyes tightly so that I should not look too covetously at the doll, and glibly ran through the prayer I knew so well.

'Gentle Jesus meek and mild,
Look upon a little child,
Pity mice in Plicity
Suffer me to come to Thee.'

I got the doll and a pat on the head. Mother, telling Father about it afterwards, said Aunty Rye looked quite impressed until I, with the doll now firmly in my possession, suddenly demanded, 'Where is Plicity?'

'Plicity?' echoed Aunty Rye bewilderedly.

'Yes,' I replied. 'Why do we have to ask Jesus to pity mice in Plicity and yet if we get mice in our larder we have to set traps to kill them?'

Mother said Aunty Rye looked as if she was going to snatch the doll away from me. It might have been better if she had, for, cradling it in my arms, I was taking it for Mother to admire when I tripped over the hearthrug, fell flat on my face and smashed the doll to smithereens. By the time my tears were dried Aunty Rye had gone and subsequently she always made sure I was out before she visited my mother. Even much later when in her capacity of Sunday school superintendent she had to present me with the prize for the best attendance during the year all I got from her was a spectral nod of recognition and a reluctant touch on my head to convey the blessing of her gloved fingers.

Though she was reputed to be frail, her will was iron and she kept her great bully of a husband in complete subjection. She interfered in almost everything he did and my parents used to mimic the meekness of his tones as he responded to her bidding. 'Yes, Rye, dear.' 'Right away, Rye, dear.' One day when Fran and I were swinging on the big iron gates of the drive, crashing them together so that they juddered on their hinges, Uncle Dick had caught us. It was not his custom to caution children and he had dragged us off roughly and boxed our ears. Fran and I had run blubbering to our respective homes, hands pressed to our stinging ears. Father was shaving at the kitchen sink, but hearing my sobs he put down the cut-throat razor and demanded to know what had happened. Father believed in chastising me with his belt across my bottom when I deserved it but he considered that only he had the right to do it and that blows on a child's ears could cause permanent damage. He was angry. Wiping the Lifebuoy lather off his face he buttoned up his shirt and put on his jacket. Mother, who had overheard my sobbed explanation, came into the kitchen.

'Where are you going?' she asked.

'To see Masher Dick,' he replied grimly.

Mother went pale. Father was thin and not very strong and Uncle Dick was known to have felled a man with one savage blow of his large fist.

'No, don't,' Mother pleaded. 'Calm down first. She's not hurt.' I bawled louder to show I was.

Father took no notice of either of us. 'I'll not have my child's ears boxed,' he said, and strode outside.

Upset by Mother's anxious face and terrified that Uncle Dick might kill Father I let my bawls erupt into screams. Mother snapped at me peremptorily and sent me upstairs. The tension was terrible until from the bedroom window I saw Father returning unscathed. He looked quite pleased with himself. I thought it safe to go downstairs.

'What happened?' Mother enquired. Her hand was clutching at the brooch that fastened the neck of her blouse.

'Nothing,' replied Father.

'What did he say?'

'I didn't see him. It was Rye who came to the door and when I asked to see him she guessed there was something wrong so she asked me to tell her what had happened. When I'd finished she just said, "He will apologise to you directly he comes back and it shall never happen again." '

Mother looked incredulous. 'I don't know how she does it but she certainly knows how to handle him,' she said.

Father resumed his shaving and a little while later a sheepishly apologetic Uncle Dick appeared at the door. He looked utterly deflated and accepted Father's recriminations with mumbled promises never to touch me again. He never did touch me again. I never swung on the gates again but it was not fear of Uncle Dick's catching me that deterred me so much as the memory of Mother's anxious face and the sight of Father striding out, as I believed, to almost certain death.

By this time Uncle Dick, whether because of dwindling finances or the inability to resist the offer of ready money, had sold a large plot of his land to the authorities for the building of a police station. It was a long red brick building divided from our drive by a high wall which enclosed a wide yard. In the yard there were kennels where lost dogs used to howl their misery for the few days they were allowed to live. On Saturdays the unclaimed ones were poisoned with prussic acid and then there might be a night or two of quiet before the kennels began to fill again with their doomed occupants. I knew it was prussic acid that was used to kill them because I was with Father in the chemist's shop on one occasion when Sergeant Zagger came in. Sergeant Zagger was a harsh, strident man. He was supposed to beat his wife and we children were terrified of him. Father was waiting for a prescription to be made up so we were able to hear what the sergeant asked for with, it seemed, gloating satisfaction. When he had made his purchase and gone, Father asked the chemist, who was a friend of his, what on earth the sergeant was buying prussic acid for.

'Oh, it's a regular order,' replied the chemist. 'It's for poisoning the lost dogs. He comes for it every Saturday.'

Father caught his breath. 'I shouldn't like his job,' he said.

'Oh, old Zagger doesn't turn a hair,' said the chemist. 'He says their howling keeps the Inspector awake and makes him bad-tempered so he's glad to get the job done.'

It was the inspector who occupied the police station and the inspector had three sons. The eldest considered Fran and me too young to be noticed but the two younger ones alternated between being our enemies and our friends. They were our enemies when they climbed up on the wall and taunted us for being girls or aimed their catapults at our bare legs; they were our friends again when, at Christmas time, they bestowed on us the unwanted beads and trinkets from their crackers. They became enemies prior to Guy Fawkes night when they threw jumping jacks over the wall or filled hollow keys with home-made gunpowder and hurled them against a stone so that they exploded with a bang; they stayed our enemies until the bonfire was ablaze when they gallantly lit our sparklers for us with matches we were not allowed to carry and invited us to a potato-pie supper in the police station followed by chasings in and out of the empty cells. The first time I was kissed by a boy was in a prison cell.

Now that Uncle Dick had a police station and a Wesleyan chapel overlooking the privacy of his grounds he seemed to tire of playing the retired gentleman. The 1914–18 war had broken out and the grocery shop gave plenty of opportunity for profiteering. He turned his attention to becoming even more prosperous. The shrubberies gave way to pigsties to provide bacon for the shop. The last fragments of green lawn disappeared beneath a curing house where the bacon was cured and the offal made into black puddings, brawn and sausages. The curing house was itself flanked by a bakery where white-overalled men and boys baked bread and pies and cakes, and soon all that remained of the once spacious grounds was the long wide driveway overlooked by regal poplars and escorted by a curved strip of garden encrusted with London Pride; an impoverished rockery and a formal fenced garden, sad with laurel bushes and plaintive with the wheezings of Gittings, the gardener. Aunty Rye stoically endured the ravaging of the grounds so long as it was necessary but as soon as the war ended she put her foot down. The pigsties were allowed to fall into disuse and the sheds became storehouses. The bakery, being far enough away from Westminster House not to be a nuisance, was let and so continued its trade; van horses continued to share the stables with the pony and the pony trap no longer had the coach-house to itself but had to make room for a delivery van that was long and black and shiny and looked more like an undertaker's deadcart than a grocery van.

All this time my parents were working and saving hard to buy their own shop. Father, in addition to working for Uncle Dick, took pupils for shorthand lessons in the evenings, and Mother, who had been a dressmaker before her marriage, took in sewing. Every penny that could be saved was put into

23

the 'Tomtit' which stood on the bobble-trimmed mantel-piece above the big kitchen range. The 'Tomtit' was a miniature wooden barrel and it had earned its peculiar name from having been the temporary resting place for a syringe which had a white rubber bulb. The bulb had pro-truded above the top of the barrel and though the juxta-position had suggested no unusual image to me or to my parents it had to a young cousin who came to visit us. As soon as she was on the threshold of the kitchen her eye had been caught by the barrel and the bulb.

'Is that a tomtit on a round of beef?' she asked.

Not knowing what a tomtit was I was only puzzled by her question but Father thought the symbolism so startlingly droll that even after the syringe was returned to its rightful home the barrel was forever afterwards referred to as 'the tomtit on the round of beef' or more usually as just the 'Tomtit'. Every so often its contents were transferred to the bank. I always knew when Father was going to the bank because he wore his Sunday suit on a weekday.

As soon as there was enough saved Father bought a house. It seemed to be a very simple transaction. A muffled little man with a quaint fragmentary moustache that looked like tea leaves clinging to his upper lip came and sat in the kitchen and drank tea. He also ate the last slice of ginger-bread which I had been coveting. Father signed his name on a cheque and the man signed a receipt. A key appeared on the table, then they both rose and shook hands; the man said goodbye and Father showed him out. Father's face was wreathed in smiles when he returned to the kitchen. He picked me up and swung me round joyfully.

'Well, Chipcart,' he said. 'We've bought our shop at last.'

'From that man?' I asked.

'Yes. Aren't you excited about it?'

I was, of course, only I wished it hadn't meant sacrificing the last slice of gingerbread.

2

Two weeks after I had told Fran my secret we said goodbye to Wesley House. The horse and wagon which were to take the furniture arrived soon after breakfast but though I begged to be allowed to stay and share in the excitement Mother was relentless. She didn't want me forever under-foot, she told Father, so I was packed off to school with the instruction that I was to go to Granny's for dinner. Normally

I looked forward to having dinner with Granny in her cosy kitchen but for once I was reluctant and the day dragged until four o'clock when Father met me outside the school gates to escort me over the level crossing which now lay between school and my new home. I had previously been taken for subdued Sunday walks past the new house, the end one of a terrace, so that I could see for myself where one day our shop was going to be, but as it was still tenanted I had never even peeped inside. Father opened the front door with a flourish.

'There you are, Chipcart,' he said cheerfully. 'Go and see what you think of it.'

I bounded in front of him like a dog off the leash and opened the first door I came to. The room was obviously the sitting room but despite the fact that the familiar furniture was arranged in much the same way as it had been at Wesley House it all looked strange and depressingly dim. Mother had made the curtains and 'dolly-tinted' them to the required shade of pale yellow before we moved and the first thing she had done that morning was to put them up so that she would not have to work under the scrutiny of curious neighbours whose windows overlooked us from across the narrow road. The living room was overlooked by more neighbours from across a back alley and the kitchen window stared straight on to a high red brick wall which enclosed a small red brick yard. I was dismayed by the smallness of the yard; there seemed barely enough space for me to wield a skipping rope. I was even more dismayed when I investigated the outside lavatory which had no window at all so that when you closed the door the only light seeped in through a gap above the door. If you left the door open you were exposed to the view of neighbours. I opened the back-yard door and peeped into the street to find myself confronted by even more houses, their 'red-raddled' doorsteps abutting the pavement, their windows densely screened by nearly identical lace curtains and over-nourished aspidistras.

On the pavement a girl was playing 'top and whip' whilst keeping a wary eye open for any sign of movement from our house. She whipped her top towards me and we exchanged shy grins. I rushed back through the yard demanding to know where I could find my top and whip.

Mother, who was still unpacking boxes of crockery, looked at me as if she wished I were a thousand miles away. 'If you think I'm going to root out toys for you you're mistaken,' she said sharply.

'Why can't you play with your ball like you were doing yesterday?' Father spoke from the step-ladder where he was trying to adjust the big temperamental wall clock so that its pendulum swung at exactly the correct rate.

'But top and whip time has come,' I wailed. 'There's a girl playing it outside on the street.'

The compulsion to play a certain game used to enslave the children of the town like a spell so that a child not able to take part in the current craze felt as out of things as an invalid or an orphan. I cannot recall if the urge beset us regularly with the seasons but seem to remember that one's bare knees and fingers felt the nip of cold when it was bowler-and-hook time; that by hopscotch time one had discarded winter boots; that marbles were played when one's hands were constantly hot and sweaty, and that top-and-whip time came when it was no longer irksome to be made to wear a jersey over one's summer dress.

Father fished in his pocket and produced twopence. 'Off you go and buy yourself a set,' he said resignedly.

I opened the yard door again and showing the girl who had smiled at me the coins asked her where she had got her top and whip.

'I'll show you,' she offered.

It was what I had hoped she would say and we skipped

27

off together, eyeing each other furtively as we went. My new acquaintance was thin and pale with limp, sparrow-brown hair and grey-flecked eyes that reminded me of frog-spawn. Waiting for me in the shop she stood submissively with shoulders hunched and arms folded like a gossiping old woman. I thought she would do for today's friend. Tomorrow I would look out for someone more promising.

My new top was orange-coloured and shaped like a carrot; the whip had a blue handle and a thin leather thong. We raced back to the side street and set our tops spinning, guiding them away from the joints between the pavement slabs and whipping them expertly when they showed signs of wobbling to a fall. My initiation into street urchinism was proving a fairly pleasurable experience. The girl and I exchanged names and ages. Hers was Cora and she was nearly three years older than I. We progressed to confiding more important snippets of information such as that her favourite sweets were chocolate rosebuds because you got a bag full to bursting for a halfpenny which was the whole of her weekly pocket money. I admitted to getting twopence a week and having four favourite kinds of sweets which led Cora to ask if she could be my very best friend. She told me that her father worked at the local steel mills which we could hear thundering and clanging somewhere beyond the rows of houses; and that on Saturday night he always ate pigs' trotters while he was reading *Pearsons Weekly*. She also told me she had a mad aunt in a lunatic asylum and a dead brother in the churchyard. Every Saturday in summer, she said, she had to walk out to where the town straggled into country and there choose a cottage with a colourful garden from which she would buy a threepenny bunch of flowers. She then had to take the flowers and arrange them on her brother's grave, so that it looked nice when churchgoers passed by on Sundays. There had been a time when she had bought a sixpenny bunch of flowers only half of which she had taken to the grave; the other half her mother had taken to the asylum for the mad aunt, but the aunt had been convinced that the flowers were for eating just like the home-baked cake and scones that were given her at the same time so the authorities had refused to allow any more.

'Haven't you got anybody dead or mad?' Cora asked in a voice that made me feel deprived.

'No, but I've got an uncle in Canada,' I countered.

Cora was not impressed. 'If your parents will let you you can come with me on Saturday to buy flowers,' she offered.

'And to the churchyard afterwards?' I begged.

Cora nodded magnanimously. 'I might let you fill one of the jam jars,' she promised.

With the prospect of such a wildly exciting day I resolved that she would have to stay my friend at least until Saturday was over.

She questioned me as to how I had spent Saturdays previously and I told her about Fran and our endless games in the stables; about the christening of dolls in the horse trough; the hole we dug at sporadically in the hope of reaching Australia; the funerals for dead fledglings.

'Stables!' ejaculated Cora, wrinkling her nose in disgust. 'Didn't they smell awful?'

'No,' I asserted. 'At least I never noticed.'

'And horse troughs and dead birds, ugh!' Her frog-spawn eyes regarded me with horror. I changed the subject quickly, panicking lest she should withdraw her invitation for Saturday. From the way she was looking at me I judged she suspected that I, like the mad aunt, might think that flowers were for eating.

When we had tired of top-spinning Cora took me on a tour round the block of houses which was her immediate playground. Everywhere, except for the tiny front gardens the size of a single bed in front of some of the houses, it was all paving stones or setts; there seemed to be no smell of earth or greenness anywhere. I wondered what games other than top and whip and perhaps ball could be played in surroundings where there was no black earth to scratch out the divisions for hopscotch or scrape a hole or ring to play marbles. Cora showed me how the pavement slabs, numbered with chalk, made ideal hopscotch divisions and explained how marbles could be played by rolling them along the gutter. The hopscotch idea seemed to be much better than anything I was used to but I knew that if ever I played 'gutter marbles' it would have to be well out of sight of my parents.

We sauntered up a wide alleyway past interminable high brick walls, pierced by chocolate-brown lozenges which were their tight-shut yard doors. Some of the doors had 'Beware of the dog' painted on them and some of the walls were encrusted with broken glass which Cora said was to discourage cats. Towards the end of the alleyway just before it rejoined the road I stopped suddenly beside the tall gabled wall of another block of houses. The wall was blank except for a discreet black door with two frosted panels; above the door hung three magnificent balls, bigger than footballs and shining like gold against the wedge of alley sky. I stared up at them entranced.

'Aren't they beautiful! I exclaimed.

'Beautiful? Pop balls?' Cora giggled and glanced about her as if looking for someone else to share such a huge joke.

'Pop balls?' I echoed, puzzled.

'Yes. They mean this is a pawn shop. Don't tell me you don't know what a pawn shop's for.'

So I didn't tell her. Neither did I tell her that however much she might deride a sign with three golden balls suspended from it I still thought it was utterly beautiful.

.   .   .   .   .

Father continued to work at Uncle Dick's shop for only about a week after we had left Wesley House when he took a job as a night watchman at a soap factory some distance away. During the day, when he wasn't sleeping, he dismantled the dilapidated wooden sheds that half filled the yard and acted as labourer to an out of work crony of his who claimed to have had some experience of bricklaying. Between them they built a neat-looking shed with slated roof and two windows, which Father insisted was to be called the 'store-room'. There were no shorthand lessons in the evenings now and as soon as tea had been cleared away and the table covered with its blue serge cloth Father spread out his volumes of *The Practical Grocer* and pored over them, turning every now and then to make carefully written notes or work at crowded columns of figures in a small black book he kept beside him.

I was a fairly precocious reader and when Father wasn't using a volume I liked to browse through it, seeking out first the delightful coloured plates which ranged from 'A rice field in Japan' to 'A prize window display in London'; from 'Salmon drifters unloading' to 'Coolies cutting sugar-cane'. There were black and white illustrations too which interested me, such as the full page of 'grocers' machines' which included things like 'tea blenders', 'fruit cleaners', 'egg testers' and 'coffee roasters and grinders' all of which were considered necessary for the aspiring grocer. The chapter headings covered every aspect of the trade from instructions on how to cut up a side of bacon to advice on the choosing of a van horse; from making soap to the blending of tobacco; from window display to the care of coach lamps. They advised on how to select and train assistants, and, deploring the passing of the 'Indenture System' whereby a boy was apprenticed to serve for five to seven years, living meantime with the grocer's family, they insisted that if the trade were to be learned thoroughly the 'short indenture' was still vitally necessary. Listed among the qualifications for a good assistant were a knowledge of how to:

Sweep the store
Arrange displays
Keep a bank account
Regulate credit
Buy stock
Look after a stable.

The recommended wage for such versatility was thirty shillings per week for a man living out; half that amount if he lived with the family. *The Practical Grocer* even gave lessons in elementary psychology in a chapter headed 'Types of customer and how to handle them' and this recommended the setting up of a 'Complaints Department' (jocularly referred to in the trade as 'The Molasses Barrel') which, acknowledging the precept that 'the customer is always right', was to be for the sole purpose of soothing and gratifying awkward customers.

The text was occasionally enlivened by little poems, and my favourite, described as being 'the work of a minor trade poet', went as follows:

'If your object be to build you up a business very large
Be certain that politeness rules the salesmen in your
    charge.
Let your customers be certain they'll always be treated
    well,
Then you'll find them ever flocking to wherever goods
    you sell.

If you wish for reputation with the people far and near,
Give good value for their money; let your statement be
    sincere.
If these lessons you will practise every day with might
    and main,
You are reasonably certain fame and fortune to obtain.'

I liked this poem so much I begged Father to copy it out in the beautiful illuminated lettering he had learned when, as a youth, he had worked in a lawyer's office. I thought it would look lovely hanging in a prominent position in the shop and would inspire the salesmen who read it. But Father only smiled and said he didn't really think poetry and provisions mixed very well and reminded me that for quite a long time he was likely to be the only salesman so it wouldn't be necessary. Anyway, he said, I had recited it so often to him he already knew it off by heart backwards.

Father leaned back to light his pipe and asked me: 'Well, and do you know all the different cuts of bacon yet?' I reeled them off: 'Gammon, ham, streaky, corner, collar, cushion, back, loin, hock, cheek.' He nodded approvingly. 'And now all the different cheeses.' I rarely omitted one or even faltered except sometimes over the pronunciation. 'Cheshire, Stilton, Cheddar, Wensleydale, Derby, Dunlop, Leicester, Gloucester, Gorgonzola, Cotherstone,' I repeated, proud of my knowledge. *The Practical Grocer* mentioned other cheeses, of course, but these were the only ones Father had come across.

'That's the ticket!' Father said, and, turning to Mother, 'You know, this girl's going to make as good a grocer as her father.' When I became too excited at the prospect and demanded to know 'how soon?' he replied cautiously, 'Some day.'

Mother said profoundly, 'Some day is bound to come someday.' She looked at the clock. 'It's long past this girl's bedtime,' she said briskly.

Father too looked at the clock as if surprised. 'By Jove! So it is! Come on, Chipcart.'

Chipcart was his pet name for me and I found myself pouting every time he used it, wishing he would call me almost anything but that. Other girls' fathers gave them delectable nicknames like 'Rosebud', 'Cherub', 'Dimplecheeks' or 'Pigeon'. Fran's parents called her 'Sweetle' but my father ridiculed such honeyed endearments and I was dubbed uncompromisingly as 'Chipcart'. It made me feel as drab as a caterpillar among a crowd of butterflies.

I slid off the chair and as Father took the stone hot-water bottle out of the oven and carried it upstairs to my bedroom I stood on the pegged hearthrug undressing lingeringly as my nightie warmed in front of the fire. Mother brought my bowl of pobs* and I ate it sitting on the wooden stool Father had made for me, while I stared at the constantly changing pictures I saw among the glowing coals. I ate my supper slowly, making it last as long as I dared, insisting, when I was exhorted to hurry, that it was far too hot even when it was hardly lukewarm.

At last Father spoke peremptorily and I had to tilt the cup and swallow the last mouthful. Going over to his chair I knelt down, clasping my hands meekly and resting my head on his knees I said my prayers. During this nightly ritual the hissing of the gaslight was the only sound allowed to disturb the reverent silence of the room.

Besides 'Gentle Jesus' I was expected to ask God to bless Father and Mother and the poor and a whole string of relations but though Father liked to hear a whisper escape from between my tight clasped hands every now and then to ensure that I hadn't fallen asleep I was not required to say my prayers audibly. They should have been very thankful I wasn't for instead of the pious supplications they believed I was repeating I was more often than not entreating the Almighty to 'make Bully Sparks fall and break his leg so that he can't walk for a year, to give my schoolteacher a sore throat so that we needn't have lessons for a week and to send a thunderbolt to strike Zagger's goat'. Bully Sparks was my chief enemy; the schoolteacher's shrill voice made lessons more like assault than instruction and Zagger's aggressive

* 'Pobs'—bread soaked in hot milk.

34

old goat made the picking of daises in Archer's field a hazardous pastime.

Before escorting me upstairs with the candle Mother stirred the fire with a poker and hung the trivet on one of the bars. On the trivet she placed two flat irons, their smooth black bases close against the red coals, ready for pressing a dress she had finished for a customer. In my bedroom the little Kelly lamp was already burning and the blind drawn. Mother tucked me into bed, went downstairs and left me to my wishing time. I was still awake and still wishing when Father came up to take the Kelly lamp.

'Father!' I called, 'when we have our shop can we have three golden balls hanging outside?'

'Three golden balls, Chipcart?' He sounded disconcerted.

'Pop balls,' I explained. 'They have them hanging outside a shop called a pawn shop down the alleyway and they're really truly beautiful.'

Father laughed and sat down on the bed while he explained what a pawn shop was and what sort of people used them, telling me funny little incidents about people pawning their Sunday clothes on Monday mornings to get a little money and then redeeming them on Saturdays ready to wear again the following Sunday. It sounded so funny that soon I was laughing too but underlying my laughter there was a sadness I had to disguise. I knew I must in future make myself despise signs with beautiful golden balls and I knew it was going to be difficult; as difficult as making myself despise exquisite flowers like dandelions just because adults said they were ugly weeds and other children scoffed at them as being 'pee the beds'.

From downstairs came the intermittent thump of flat irons on the table, the noise of the fire being stirred again and again. Later the smell of fried bacon was wafted up the stairs and into my room and I knew Father must be having his supper before setting out on the long cycle ride to the

35

factory. I heard him go outside to the storeroom and guessed that he was filling his acetylene lamp with carbide. When that was done he would sit down and wind his puttees over his trousers before wheeling his bicycle out into the yard. I heard the back door open and Mother's murmured goodbye; I heard the bell being tested and then the one impelling scud of his foot on the pavement as he started off. I started to wish again. This time it was that we could soon open our shop so that Father wouldn't have to work at night while Mother and I slept safe in our beds.

3

It came as a surprise returning home from school one day to find the parlour door wide open on to an empty room. I stood on the threshold astonished. Gone was the red plush sofa that had so often been my daybed during the small ailments of childhood; gone were the mirrored overmantle from above the fireplace and the brass fender and fire irons. The cross-legged bamboo table had disappeared from in front of the window along with its burden of aspidistra; the picture of Grandfather no longer accused me from the wall; the carpet was gone and so was the deep fur hearthrug in whose embrace I was used to sobbing out my hurts and tantrums. I ran into the kitchen, noticing with dismay that one of the easy chairs from the parlour had replaced the paisley-cushioned rocking chair where in earlier childhood I had night after night nestled against Father and been lulled into drowsiness by a combination of rocking and the unflagging narration of stories about a little boy called Bobbie Dawson. Bobbie Dawson had epitomised all stupid silly and naughty children and his misdeeds and punishments were intended to convey to me the likely consequences should I ever behave like anything but a good little girl.

Father was out but Mother was busy at the sink.

'Where's everything?' I demanded anxiously.

'Sold!' Mother replied, and seeing my perplexity added with a smile, 'You can't have sitting-room furniture in a shop now, can you?'

'Are we really going to have our shop at last?'

'Indeed we are,' she replied. 'Father's away seeing the builders at this minute.'

I rushed back to the parlour and there stood in the centre of the bare room not knowing whether the involuntary twitching of my lips threatened pouts or smiles. It was dreadful to think of our furniture gracing someone else's home, of our chairs being sat upon by strange people in strange houses, and yet even I could not deny the promise of the empty room. It was really beginning to look a little like a shop already. I tried to imagine myself behind a counter, greeting customers, weighing out purchases. By the time Father came home I was singing loudly and jumping about on the bare wood floors revelling in the unaccustomed echoes.

The following week a gang of men arrived from the Electricity Company and set to work digging up the road and part of the pavement, ready for the thick rope of cable that was trundled along on an enormous reel. We were the first people to have electricity in the area and the preparations for its installation attracted a more dedicated audience than a herb doctor at the local market or an evangelist at a street corner. For three days the men dug and pick-axed and laid cable, watched from a safe distance by the habitual 'out of works' and 'on the clubs' who waited with comatose persistence in the hope that the dangerous experiment would explode or at least make a big flash and thus bear out all their muttered prognostications. But no such eventuality occurred; the patch of road was re-surfaced, the pavement re-laid and the 'out of works' and 'on the clubs' shuffled back to their lamp-posts.

As soon as the Electricity Company had finished the builders came to demolish the low wall and to cement over the tiny garden that separated the front of the house from the pavement. The two sash windows were replaced by a large plate-glass window and then the busy, whistling men turned their attention to knocking out the wall that divided the lobby from the parlour. The front door gave way to a new glass-panelled one which now opened directly into the shop thus making it necessary for the straight staircase to be re-placed by a sharply curving one which led into the living room. After the decorators had splashed whitewash around and covered the flowery patterned wall with a paper that simulated blue and white tiles the effect was one of clean, cool spaciousness and only the ornamental ceiling rose and a rectangle of hearth tiles against one wall remained to betray the fact that the shop had once been our parlour. It was not long before the blue and white tiled paper disappeared behind tiers of shelves; shallow shelves for displaying jams and bottled fruits; deep ones for loaves; racked ones for eggs. The counter was installed; a huge 'L'-shaped bulk of mahogany stained as dark as old port with fancy flutings in front and a marble slab covering the section where the bacon would be cut and butter patted into shape.

'Strong enough for you to dance on,' said Mr Josh who had built the counter. He lifted me up on to it and joyfully I danced a few steps until I caught Father's disapproving eye when I clambered down self-consciously. Bobbie Dawson had got into trouble for just standing on his mother's precious new table and I supposed a new counter must be regarded as being precious too.

'Good for a hundred years,' affirmed Mr Josh, thumping at the counter with his clenched fist as if daring the wood to retaliate with the faintest creak of protest. 'And solid!' he went on, 'solid as a pavement that there counter is.'

'You're right about that,' Father agreed dutifully.

Mr Josh stood back gratified. To him solidness was synonymous with beauty. If anyone had asked Mr Josh to make them a reproduction piece of Chippendale it would have turned out to be as robust as a railway wagon. 'I can't abide flimsy-flamsy,' he used to say, over and over again, and as a consequence everything he made could be guaranteed to stand up to unremitting use and abuse for at least ten decades. His humour was of the same calibre and he never visited us without making an opportunity to crack all three of the jokes which comprised the repertoire of a lifetime. When we knew Mr Josh was coming Father told me severely: 'Now try not to laugh at any of his jokes. It just encourages him.' But Mr Josh needed no encouragement from me. As soon as the business of the counter was settled he produced a pipe like a piece of tree bark and taking a large jack-knife from his pocket he started to shave tobacco off a thick black wedge that seemed to be permanently rooted in his rutty palm.

'I see by the paper there's a woman been killed in Birkenhead,' he began.

Father flashed me a warning look. We both knew what was coming.

'Aye?' said Father, with only a fractional amount of interest. I pretended to look through the window which had been whitened over to prevent 'folks gawping'.

Mr Josh, confident that we were both agog with interest, rubbed out the tobacco between his fingers, making us wait for his scintillating explanation of how the woman had been killed. It was at this juncture that I usually obliged Mr Josh by bursting out with an interrogative 'How?' but remembering Father's warning I kept quiet. The silence seemed a little longer than usual but at last Mr Josh deemed it had continued long enough.

'I believe somebody stabbed her with the mangle,' he elucidated and immediately gripped his pipe between his teeth to disguise his mirth. Father grunted. I stifled a giggle. I couldn't help it. I always did think Mr Josh's three jokes were funny no matter how often I heard them.

Father tried to steer the conversation to another subject by mentioning a friend of his who had just won five pounds in a football sweep. But Mr Josh was determined to embark on his second joke and Father's remark gave him his opportunity.

'He has now, has he? That's why he's been dashing around as daft as a spider on a hearth, is it?' He took out his pipe and pointed the stem at Father. 'You want to tell him he should be more careful and look where he's going or he'll be getting himself run over by the brickworks chimney.'

By this time Father had begun to get a hunted look in his eyes. He moved towards the living-room door as if ready to finish work for the night. Mr Josh lingered relentlessly awaiting the right moment to perpetrate his third and final masterpiece. It came as always as he was putting on his jacket preparatory to taking his leave. 'I saw Savage Annie the other night,' he announced.

Father, relieved that the last joke was under way, evinced a little more interest. 'Did you?' he said almost jubilantly.

41

'Aye, and I'll bet you don't know what she was up to?'

We knew, oh, how well we knew what Savage Annie, who in fact had been dead for some years, had been up to in Mr Josh's imagination, but we never spoiled this moment for him.

'No,' said Father. 'What was it this time?'

I stared at Mr Josh, my lips involuntarily forming the words I knew he was about to utter.

'The silly old faggot was knitting a jumper using two bars of soap for needles.' Wheezing and shaking with suppressed laughter Mr Josh gripped the handle of the door ready to let himself out but as always he paused on the threshold and addressed me.

'Now, young miss, remember what I've always told you never to do!' he adjured me.

'What?' I asked with feigned innocence. Again I knew what was coming but I knew that nothing would stop him saying it.

'Never you pick a guinea pig up by its tail or its eyes will fall out.'

It used to distress me that Mr Josh should think it necessary to remind me every time he came and I used to assure him repeatedly that I would never dream of treating a guinea pig so cruelly. It was not until many years later that I discovered that this parting shot was really Mr Josh's fourth joke.

Father's sigh of relief coincided with the slamming of the outside door and was almost as loud. 'Stabbed her with the mangle!' he muttered bitterly.

I changed my grin to a sneer before I looked at him. 'I wonder how many times Mr Josh has told those jokes?' I said ingratiatingly.

'How many days are there in a year?' replied Father glumly.

'Three hundred and sixty-five.'

'Well, Mr Josh is about sixty so multiply three hundred and sixty-five by sixty and then treble it and you'll get some sort of an idea,' said Father.

Mother came in from the living room just as he was giving the shop a final survey. 'My goodness!' she said, eyeing the counter, and looked at Father to see if she should comment approvingly or otherwise. He gave her no help.

'Mr Josh says it's solid as a pavement and good for a hundred years,' I burst out excitedly.

'What do you think of it?' Mother asked.

Father's mouth twisted wryly. 'He's used three times as much wood as he needed to have and charged accordingly.'

'You think it's too clumsy?' Mother sounded anxious.

'Well, at least there's nothing will shift it.' Father's grin broadened to a smile. 'I daresay it's my own fault. I should have explained to him that I only wanted to cut the bacon with a knife, not a pickaxe.'

Mother smiled back at him. 'Well, it's ready for business and that's a comfort,' she said.

'Aye,' agreed Father. He gave the counter a tolerant slap. 'And from the look of it it'll stand up to some mighty good business.'

Mother became brisk. 'Come along, Chipcart,' she urged me. 'You've got to try on your new coat if you're coming with us to Liverpool tomorrow.'

I grimaced behind my hands. I loved new clothes but I hated the repeated fittings I had to endure.

'Another new coat?' Father expostulated with a glower.

'Yes, I've nearly finished it. It's only the setting of the buttons I have to do now.'

'Why can't she go in her Sunday coat?' Father argued. 'It looked all right last time she wore it.'

'She had to wear her Sunday coat for school on Monday

43

while I mended her other one and she ruined it in just that one day.'

'She ruins too many clothes,' said Father, glowering at me again.

There was no denying I was hard on my clothes. Rusty nails rent them; any mud I fell into was always of a kind that stained ineradicably and even grass was not colour fast when I sat on it. Father began clearing his throat as he followed Mother and me through to the living room and I pretended an urgent need for the lavatory to escape another lecture about my destructiveness with my clothes. The last one had been memorable. I had come home from school with yet another dress irrevocably torn. Mother had cried when she saw it, but Father, instead of being angry, had taken me on his knee and explained how hard Mother had to work nowadays and how, to keep me nicely dressed, she was ready 'to work her fingers to the bone'. Other children who weren't lucky enough to have dressmakers for mothers, he said, simply couldn't have a succession of new clothes as I had and so they took care of them and made them last a long time. The prospect of my bed being made and my food being prepared by a mother who had only gory red bones instead of fingers so affected me that I promised in future to take the greatest care of my attire and the next time I was arrayed in a new dress I was so fearful of spoiling it that I spent a miserable day as a spectator rather than a participant in the games my friends played. Still relatively spotless at the end of the day I skipped home to enjoy my parents' commendations on my achievement. Just outside the house there was a lamp-post and so exuberant was my mood that I threw my arms about it and swung round once, twice. I almost screamed as I tore myself away from it. The lamp-post had been newly painted with dark brown paint. Mother scolded. I sulked. Father, when he heard about it, gave me a long sorrowful look that was worse than any whipping.

'You can dress her in a sugar sack tomorrow,' he had told Mother.

I had cried myself to sleep that night, visualising the reactions of the girls when I turned up in a dress made from a sugar sack with the words 'Finest Gran.' or 'Coarse Demerara' printed all over it in large black letters. I wondered if I could indulge in one of my 'quarter to nine pains' as Father called them. School started at nine o'clock and these pains afflicted me frequently during term time at about twenty minutes to nine, and continued agonisingly until a quarter past nine by which time the school attendance register would have closed for the day and the pains could be miraculously assuaged by the consumption of iced cakes and chocolate biscuits. I had awakened next morning prepared to be too ill to eat my breakfast but when I sat up and looked at the chair on which my clothes were placed there was no dreaded sugar sack for me to wear but a new dress made from the bodice and skirt of two old ones. I put it on and looking at myself in the wardrobe mirror decided it was endurable. In fact if in the past I had not heard Mother making disparaging remarks about other children having to wear such makeshift dresses I think I should have been rather pleased with it.

Tonight, however, I was to escape another lecture. When I got back from the lavatory Father was stropping his razor in the kitchen but he was not singing as he usually did when preparing to shave. I realised that a lecture was still possible so I stood more docilely than usual, obeying Mother's instructions to 'lift up this arm' or 'straighten up' while she inspected the length and marked the buttonholes for my coat. It took a long time and I began to yawn.

Mother sat back on her heels and looked at me crossly. 'Don't you want to come to Liverpool?' she demanded.

'Yes,' I said quickly. We were all going to Liverpool to

buy fittings and stock for the shop and I'd been nearly bursting with excitement for days.

'Well just keep still or you'll be spending the day with Granny instead,' Mother threatened.

Father's voice called from the kitchen. 'Smack her if she's not behaving.'

I stood so still I thought I might die with not breathing and I stood still again later without murmuring while Mother tortured my hair into curls and tied them up with strips of rag.

'Now go to sleep straight away,' said Mother when she had tucked me in. 'You've got a tiring day in front of you tomorrow.'

I was so obedient that I found I had only just time to take out the hated curling rags before sleep overcame me

. . . .

My parents looked very smart in their best clothes and I believed that even I looked quite fetching when we set out to catch the eight-thirty train to Liverpool. Mother had suggested we go on the seven-thirty train and so qualify for cheap workman's tickets, but Father was firm. He was not going to have his day's outing spoiled by starting it with a rush. At the station a scattering of passengers, mostly identifiable by their crutches, bandages or eyeshades as outpatients *en route* for treatment at Liverpool hospitals, slid us wispy smiles; the little porter, always known as 'Birdseed', gave us a cluck of greeting; the booking clerk's voice crackled affably through the aperture and when we emerged from the booking office the lordly station-master was there to offer a cordial handshake. When the train came in, dead on time, the fireman saluted us with the wave of an oily rag while the engine driver's smudgy face grinned at us through a cloud of steam. It was always like this when Father went anywhere.

He seemed to know so many people. Even on Sunday-afternoon walks when everyone, particularly the brethren of the church and chapel, were being so self-consciously good that they were loath to shape their lips into anything that couldn't be construed as a prayer, Father was constantly raising his silver-knobbed walking stick or lifting his trilby hat in acknowledgment of innumerable acquaintances. I always tried to walk proudly when I was out with Father, so much so that he had sometimes to reprove me with a half-jocular 'Stop that silly begger business, Chipcart!' When I responded by slumping and dragging my feet there would come a much crisper rebuke.

The porter was closing the compartment doors at the far end of the train but my parents lingered until all the hospital patients had settled into their seats before ushering me quickly into an empty compartment. This strategy was to save us from being cooped up with liniment-soaked bodies, which Father abhorred, and from being regaled during the journey with plaintive chronicles of illnesses or accidents. It also saved us from being saddled with the task of escorting some of the halt and lame up the pier to the tramcar when we reached our destination. My parents were not callous about illness or infirmity. Indeed there was nothing Mother liked better than to be seen taking a jug of her special invalid gruel to a neighbour who was confined to bed and both Father and Mother could, if necessary, be courageous listeners to the most morbid descriptions of ailments. It was just that they preferred the sufferers to have either recovered or died before they heard about them so that the narrative was safely in the past tense.

The guard appeared at the open window with an amiable 'How yer, Bob!' for Father and, catching sight of me, informed my parents with great familiarity that they didn't smack my bottom often enough. I scowled at him from my corner but he seemed bent on blighting my whole day by revealing the secret of my latest misdemeanour. (I suspected he had observed me and Cora pinching the station-master's rhubarb from the siding beds.) Mercifully, after the initial, 'I'll tell you what she was up to,' interspersed with heavy winks, a shout from 'Birdseed' recalled him to his duty. He turned away, gave a compliant blast of his whistle, a wave of his green flag and as the train tightened itself for the journey I was thankful to see his leering face slide away from the window.

At Birkenhead we hurried from the station to join the queue already at the turnstiles and once through we headed with the throng of travellers to board the ferry. Mother stayed below in the saloon where it was warm, but Father and I climbed the iron staircase to the top deck where we had to duck to the breeze and Father had to hold on to his expensive new trilby. My own hat was secured by a band of elastic under my chin—secured so tightly that it had already cut into my throat like a brand. On board there was a good contingent of office workers whose feet beat a staccato accompaniment to the muffled throb of the engines as they marched round and round the deck with the dedicated air of having pledged themselves to walk a certain number of steps before the boat reached the Liverpool landing stage. Father and I leaned on the rail, delighting in every aspect of the river's pageantry: the ferry boat's pulsing propeller churning the sludgy water into gravy brown foam; the bossy tugs; a paddle boat which chafed the sluggish rhythm of the waves as its fretful siren chafed the air. Across the water the Liver buildings loomed, hoary against a slate-grey sky, overlooking dark, huddled warehouses patterned by crane jibs and spiky masts; the docks and wharfs were like a maze from which protruded the disembodied funnels of ships undergoing refit; big liners rested somnolently at their temporary berths. The ferry took us close to a liner moored in mid river waiting for tugs and tide. With mounting excitement Father and I spelled out her name to each other —'R E G I N A'. It was the very liner on which, only months earlier, Father's brother, my Uncle Wallace and his wife, Jinny, had returned to Canada after spending a holiday with us. I had been allowed to go with my parents to see them off and never before had I waved goodbye with so much enthusiasm. They had stayed with us for three weeks and during that time Mother, who was aware that Father's family considered themselves a cut above her, had been determined to impress them with our gentility. The best cutlery had been used at every meal; the Dutch oven on which the breakfast bacon was usually cooked in front of the kitchen fire was banished to the shed and the breakfast cooked in a frying pan on the gas stove; a new pegged rug, made by Mother the previous winter but stored under a bed until now, was spread on the floor and white linen drug-geting was laid over the shabby staircarpet. For me, life had been as restricted as if I had been wearing a harness. Un-suitable playmates—virtually everyone I knew—had been forbidden the vicinity of the house. I had been compelled to wear my best clothes every day and frowned and threatened into being on my best behaviour every waking minute. At teatime I had been required to eat thin bread and butter in-stead of the thick bread and dripping I found so much tastier and when from time to time I had been on the point of betraying that this was not my normal fare Mother's glare had been almost enough to make me lose my appetite. At night I had been sent to bed an hour earlier than my usual time and sternly discouraged from singing myself to sleep. Every morning I had been warned that I must attend to the calls of nature as soon as the desire manifested itself because, it was explained, with strangers in the house, to delay until the need became frantically urgent and then go flinging myself at the lavatory door demanding the immediate vacation of the occupant, or else, might lead to shameful

49

consequences. After the first few days of Uncle Wallace's visit I began discreetly quizzing as to when he was going back to Canada, and when the happy day came, after I'd remembered my manners and hoped they had enjoyed their stay, I had sung all the way to the ship. There was a brass band playing on the landing stage, the lines of bunting dancing in the breeze and the general festive air of the crowd of well-wishers had reflected my own mood of elation at the departure of our guests.

I think my parents too had been glad to see them go. The incompatibility had become apparent as soon as Mother discovered that Aunt Jinny used face powder and wore thin, sleeveless silk nightdresses and lacy underwear. She not only wore such garments but exhibited them on the high clothes line normally reserved for sheets and tablecloths. Mother considered a nightdress should be a thoroughly opaque tent of white flannelette or cambric with perhaps a decorative needlework frill at neck and wrists, and even these, along with fleecy bloomers and stays, were hung on a discreetly low line after the milkman had made his morning delivery. They were always taken in again, dry or not, before the milkman called again on his evening round. Mother was very worried about the effect Aunt Jinny's apparel might have on the milkman. I thought she was afraid he might start watering down the milk.

The dissimilarity in outlook became even more apparent when Uncle Wallace and Aunt Jinny had attended with Mother a function advertised as a 'Whist Drive and Dance'. Mother loved whist drives but both she and Father denounced dancing as 'Devil's Capers', so she was always careful to leave as soon as the whist playing was finished. To Mother's mortification, however, Uncle Wallace and his wife had taken it for granted that they would stay for the dancing and stay they did, enjoying themselves hugely until the dance ended at five minutes to midnight, an unprecedented hour for Mother, who had felt constrained to remain as chaperon to her guests. Father, who didn't approve of whist drives when they were held in a hall used for dancing, took the attitude that Mother had only herself to blame for taking them, which made Mother even more embittered. She went around with her thin lips as down-curved as a bucket handle for a least a week afterwards.

There had been a good deal of head-shaking after the final departure of Uncle Wallace and Aunt Jinny.

'If that's what Canada does for people I don't want to go there,' said Father.

'I don't suppose we'll ever be invited,' replied Mother. She was right. We never heard from them again.

4

The ferry boat neared the Liverpool landing stage and sent the grey-brown water leaping at the exposed piles with their permanent encrustation of nightmarish slime. We prepared ourselves for the inevitable bump and watched the hawsers thrown out, caught expertly and looped round bollards; the two gangplanks went down with simultaneous crashes and the passengers surged off the boat. The tide was out and the gangway steeply inclined so that by the time many of the passengers had reached the top they were too breathless to thwart the importunate newspaper boys and buttonhole sellers who converged on them like starlings on stubble. We dodged them and came out on to the wide pavement where we stood savouring the bustle of the city; the chaos of tramcars which slid and clanged along a complexity of tracks that thinned into parallel pairs as they reached the shadowed roads separating the tall buildings; teams of carthorses straining at loaded wagons, their feet slithering on the setts as they toiled to obey the whips and exhortations of their drivers; cabbies delivering or awaiting passengers; porters racing with handcarts, top-heavy with luggage, towards the blaring steamers; bootblacks with their Cherry Blossom footrests at the kerbside, and, plodding along the gutter, a dejected troupe of sandwich men, their boards blazoning promises of a three-course meal for ninepence; a rock-bottom sale; the cheapest haircut and shave in town and punishment for the ungodly. Amidst the bustle stood a tall helmeted policeman who, from a small dais which enclosed his lower half like a dustbin, majestically controlled the maelstrom of traffic. For Father and me the traffic policeman was one of the most enthralling sights Liverpool had to offer and at home we often vied with each other in imitating the agility of his signals.

'Come along!' said Mother impatiently, giving me a push, and when I stumbled she added, 'And for goodness' sake stop staring at the sky and look where you're putting your feet.' I tore my gaze from the lonely Liver birds so high above me and looking so cold I used to wish the mayor would command they should be given feathers or fur coats. We climbed aboard a waiting tramcar and settled ourselves on the shiny wooden seats which were perforated like colanders. I slid down and crouched beneath my seat holding out my hand so that the light shining through the holes spotted my glove. Like a

53

ladybeetle, I was thinking, when a tug from Mother hauled me back to my seat. I looked at the other passengers to see if they had witnessed her action. Mother always did something to make me shy and ashamed when I was out with her. Father called my attention to the tram driver who was cleaning the points by digging at the tram line with a slim metal rod. When he had finished he slipped the rod into a socket at the side of the tram, mounted his wooden platform and grasped the steering handles with gauntleted hands. In response to the conductor's double pull at the leather straps that ran like a pair of reins from the rear of the tram to the platform the driver jangled a large bell suspended above his head. The bell was intended to warn traffic and pedestrians that we were about to move off and when the warning was not immediately heeded both driver and conductor reinforced it with loud recriminatory bellows. Squeaking and juddering and watched by glowering stone statues the tram slid away from the confusion of the pierhead towards the more ordered busyness of the main shopping centres.

I stared at the many-windowed shops and the kerbside hawkers who displayed every kind of small merchandise: some offered farthings with the whole of the Lord's Prayer engraved on one side; others hat pins at a penny for a bundle of four; there were trays of brightly coloured hair slides and hat ornaments; toy birds which fluttered at the end of a string; Dutch-clogged dolls that walked at the end of a stick. There were flower sellers, shawl-clad women with large baskets or perambulators stuffed full of fresh flowers who pushed selected bunches urgently under the noses of passers-by. Wherever there was space there was a fruit barrow piled pyramid fashion and attended by more shawl-clad women whose piercingly reiterated cries of 'Ripe tomatoes, threepence a pound, all sound' assaulted the tram-car each time it halted. Among the seething crowds of shoppers troupes of barefooted men and women porters, arms akimbo, tiered baskets high on their heads, threaded their graceful, epithet-cleared way towards the marketplace. At nearly every street corner there was a barrel-organ or 'hurdy-gurdy', as we called them, with the proprietor doggedly mangling out its repertoire while a woman shook an empty cap pleadingly towards the crowds. Sometimes there was a sad little monkey chained to the hurdy-gurdy valiantly attempting to dance to the music; and once, instead of a woman soliciting for alms, it was a forlorn-looking mongrel dog which sat as rigidly as one of the stone statues with the cap gripped between its jaws.

The tram deposited us at the entrance to a narrow street which led away from the main thoroughfare and Father turned off into an even narrower side street lined with the blank windows of wholesale warehouses. He pushed open a door and we entered the quiet, sawdust-carpeted store of the scale maker. Here on broad shelves were scales designed for every type of trade: butchers, bakers, grocers, confectioners, fruiterers, chandlers, tobacconists and fish merchants, while in the dim back premises leather-aproned men filed at or polished and assembled scale components and inserted or extracted tiny pieces of lead at the base of the weights as they tested them for accuracy. An old man detached himself from the gloom and hobbled forward. Father explained what he wanted and the old man shakily lifted a handsome brass scale from one of the shelves and placed it on the bench for Father's inspection. His bent fingers seemed reluctant to leave the scale and moved caressingly up and down the polished centre beam, slid over the burnished weight pan and the chains from which it was suspended; they wiped a speck of dust from the white marble slab. With similar affection he placed the weights on the bench in a gleaming, diminishing row from seven pounds to a quarter of an ounce. The weights were broad based and thin-waisted with handles that you could slip your fingers through and standing there on the bench they reminded me of a row of knights in golden armour; I began to christen them with the names of knights from the Round Table. Father said he would buy the scale and to my relief the old man seemed pleased; I had begun to think he was too fond of it to let it go. Next Father bought a scale for weighing potatoes, but as it was squat and painted black and had only a large tin scoop I lost interest and wandered off to inspect more closely what the workmen were doing. When I returned Father was buying yet another scale. It was again a brass one but it was smaller and neater than the first and its weights were round and flat so that they nestled one into another. The biggest weight was a pound. I guessed it would be for weighing sweets and immediately began to fondle it as the old man had fondled the big scale. He looked at me benignly.

'You like that one, do you?' he asked.

I smiled at him. 'I think it's a dear little scale.'

'Good,' said Father. 'You can have the job of polishing it every Saturday morning. That'll keep you out of mischief.' I wished I had kept my fingers to myself, particularly when I learned later it was intended for weighing out tobacco, not sweets.

We left the scale-maker's and made our way to another warehouse where Father bought a tradesman's bicycle and a couple of baskets that fitted in to a carrier in front of the handlebars, and left instructions for the lettering of the metal advertising plate which was to be fixed under the crossbar. He ordered a sack truck and then toured the warehouse, choosing scoops of different sizes; faucets for barrels; butter pats; bacon knives and saws, and white enamelled display trays. The assistant produced a box of spiked display tickets in white enamel with black lettering.

'Here you are,' said Father to me, indicating the box. 'You just sort out which of these you think we'll need while your mother and I go and look at a few other things.' I knew

I was being disposed of temporarily but with such an important job to do I made no objection. I bent lovingly over the box, selecting first what I knew were the essential tickets like 'Pure Lard' and 'Finest Butter' and 'Best Margarine', but then I let myself be more adventurous and put out tickets which proclaimed 'Nothing Finer', 'Very Choice', 'Fine Eating', and 'Has No Rival', and one which particularly caught my fancy. It was worded 'Flavour, Fragrance, Strength'. When Father came back he discarded all but the most essential ones, throwing the rest back into the box. I rooted out the 'Flavour, Fragrance, Strength' again and held it in front of him, believing that he couldn't have noticed it. 'Not this one?' I asked eagerly.

There was amusement in Father's eyes as he studied the ticket. 'Now what on earth are you thinking we could put that ticket on?' he asked banteringly. I was ready for his question having already posed it to an assistant.

'Tea!' I rejoined pertly. 'Don't you see? "Flavour, Fragrance, Strength".'

Father took the ticket from me and put it firmly back into the box. 'I see that if we put that ticket on our tea, Chipcart, we wouldn't sell any because the customers would be sure it was made from senna pods. Come along. We've finished here.'

'What now?' asked Mother when we came out again into the street.

'Food!' pronounced Father. 'I'm hungry and I'll bet Chipcart is.'

I nodded jubilantly. I was always hungry and eating at a café was a rare enough treat.

'A cup of tea will do for me,' said Mother pallidly. 'We can eat when we get home.'

My spirits sank. Mother begrudged money on eating out and when she took me to a café no matter how near I was to starving I had to be content with a cup of tea and a toasted teacake served by an indifferent waitress who sensed she needn't expect a tip.

'Well, it won't do for me,' Father said. 'I want something that's either looked over a hedge or under a gate. It'll be a while before we get home.'

It was a smiling waitress who brought us the menu and took our order for three-course dinners followed by 'gallons of tea'. Mother tried to demur once more but Father ignored her and she subsided with a long-suffering smile. When the food came she still pretended she had no appetite, but her plate was cleaned and she was laying down her knife and fork almost as soon as Father and me.

'I told you you'd be hungry,' teased Father.

'I wasn't hungry,' she countered. 'But I wasn't going to leave it for them to serve to somebody else.' She pursed her lips primly. 'But I'd sooner have waited till I got home.'

After dinner it was time to go to a paper merchant's store which was as colourful as an artist's studio with the many different papers that filled the shelves. We chose bags first: the traditional blue ones for sugar; brown ones for oatmeal and barley; white for flour. Father turned his attention to inspecting the different qualities of greaseproof paper for the first wrappings of bacon and butter and next he fingered the thick creamy-coloured paper known as 'White Cap', assessing its smoothness. Butter and bacon were never sold without these two wrappings and both papers had to be completely devoid of printing knowing from experience that housewives suspected the ink might poison the butter. He bought tissue paper for wrappings bread; white glossy paper known as 'demi-tea', which, as its name suggests, was for packaging tea. Finally he and Mother chose various colours of thick matt paper for dried fruits and once again tradition influenced their choice. Currants were sold usually in maroon-coloured paper; sultanas, yellow; raisins, blue. It was lovely paper, just like the drawing paper we used at school.

'Well, that's the lot,' said Father at last.

Back in the busy shopping centre the shop windows were now fully lit; the pavements even more crowded; the kerb-side hawkers more urgently entreating, the scudding trams more frequent.

I was relieved when we boarded the tramcar to return to the ferry; my best shoes were pinching and I was hungry again. We were passing St George's Hall guarded by its crouching stone lions when Father asked:

'Enjoyed yourself, Chipcart?'

I nodded.

'How would you like to have a shop in Liverpool and live here all the time?'

It had never occurred to me before that people lived in Liverpool; that there were homes behind the big shops and grimy docks and warehouses. I shook my head emphatically.

'Why not?' persisted Father. 'And speak up! Only babies shake heads when they're asked a question.'

'I'd be frightened,' I told him.

'Silly girl!' He dismissed me and turned to mother.

I knew I wasn't being silly. Mr Josh had once told me that every night when the town clock struck thirteen the stone lions got down from their pillars and prowled around the town and despite his assurance that they never molested anyone and that it was by arrangement with Liverpool Corporation that the crouching lions were allowed this hour of liberty to stretch their cramped legs I was desperately anxious to get away from the city at the first signs of darkness. I just didn't trust stone lions.

5

Two days later Father stood surveying the stock which so
far comprised only a few cartons of cigarettes, a box of
clothes pegs and two large glass jars of pickled onions which
Mother herself had prepared and which stood invitingly on
the counter with their china ladles in readiness. That morning
the postman had delivered a parcel containing white drill
jackets and aprons for Father and a white coat for Mother

and later on a handcart from the local timber yard had brought a bag full of piny smelling fresh sawdust for strewing on the bare wood floor of the shop. Father, impatient to put his enterprise to the test and undeterred by the empty shelves, said suddenly:

'I think we'll open up tomorrow.'

Mother looked startled. 'There's not much to sell,' she told him.

'I can call at the bakery on my way to work tonight and tell him to deliver first thing in the morning. He'll be glad to get started.'

Father had already contacted an obscure little bakery in the dockside area of the town which was accustomed to catering for the lusty appetites of barge and boat crews and when he had satisified himself as to cleanliness and sampled its cakes and custard pies, noting their size, he had agreed to place an order.

Mother and I were up to greet Father home from work next morning and immediately after breakfast Father donned his smart new jacket and apron. The day promised to be full of excitement.

'Please, Father, may I spread the sawdust on the floor?' I begged when I saw him filling a pail from the sack. He looked as if he were going to refuse so I put on my accomplished wheedle. 'Please.'

'You can try,' he compromised. 'But it's not so easy as it looks, you know.'

I plunged my hands into the pail and scattered sawdust on the floor. It lay lumpily and not at all like the golden coverlet I was striving to achieve. I attempted to fill the bare spaces.

'That's enough,' said Father. 'You're just making a mess of it.' He got a bottle of water and sprinkled it over the sawdust before sweeping the floor with a broom.

'Now watch me!' he instructed. 'There's a knack to this

job, you'll find.' He spread the sawdust with the ease of long practice; when he had finished the floor was hidden beneath a smooth golden carpet.

The baker's horse-drawn cart arrived simultaneously with the opening of the shop door and the trays of cakes warm and fresh from the ovens were carried in filling the shop with their mouth-watering fragrance. Even so soon after breakfast I felt hungry again. Father slid the full trays into the window and we went outside to see how they looked. There were butter-yellow sponge cakes cloaked with pink and white icing, snowy with coconut and tipped with half-cherries; ginger cakes frosted with sugar; toast-brown pastry cups full of golden custard and freckled with spice. Father mixed some whiting and wrote on the window 'Monster cakes and custards only one penny each' and then waited tensely for customers. The surprise opening of the shop proved in itself to be an attraction and customers came quickly enough, buying perhaps only one cake and one custard at first but soon hurrying back with plates and dishes for half a dozen or more. A boy newly left school came to ask for a job as errand boy and, being taken on immediately, was kept busy trotting to and from the bakery—virtually from one end of the town to the other—bringing basketfuls of cakes to replenish the quickly disappearing stocks while customers leaving with full plates met intending customers with empty plates and complimented one another on having found such good value. And they were good value, those cakes and pies, twice as big for a penny as those sold by other shops in the vicinity. Even I, with the appetite of an Irish navvy, could only manage one at a sitting.

When, a few days after the opening of the shop, I was allowed to celebrate my birthday with a party Mother cut the baker's cakes into quarters before she placed them on the table. I overheard Father chiding her on over-economy but Mother only tossed her head and said she wasn't going to let other people's children make pigs of themselves in her house. 'All Chipcart's friends are bound to have eyes bigger than their bellies,' she said. Father grunted something about meanness and I felt ashamed of Mother, expecting my friends to taunt me after the party with remarks about 'quarter-cakes'. I ought to have known that Father would have his own way of dealing with the situation. While I and my guests were still at the compulsory bread and butter and sandwich stage of the birthday tea a dog who had followed one of the girls whined at the back door. Father let him in.

'I wonder if the dog likes cakes?' he asked and offered it one of the quarters. It disappeared in one swallow. He offered it another. Save for Mother everyone screamed with laughter as they saw the dog's eyes cross when they focussed on the cake held so close to its nose and the ensuing quick gulp but our laughter thinned as we saw the cakes being fed to the dog one by one until the dish was quite empty. Father opened his eyes wide in pretended surprise.

'Well, the greedy dog's eaten the lot!' he exclaimed. 'I'd better go and get some more.' He went into the shop and returned with the plate piled high with whole cakes. The reaction of my friends was almost as quick as the dog's. When the party was over and my guests had gone home Mother said reproachfully·

'You shouldn't have done that. We shall have their parents complaining their kids have been sick in the night and not fit to go to school.' Father looked so remorseful that the next day I bounded in from school, eager to reassure them that not one of my friends had been sick and that all of them had enjoyed the party.

'Not one of them was sick?' Mother asked. She sounded disappointed.

'Not one!' I stressed gleefully. 'But Mary's dog was, terribly.'

The baker's pies and cakes proved something of a nine days' wonder and by then people became as tired of buying them as Father was of selling them. The main stock had now arrived; the window was dressed and the shelves packed full and he was anxious to get on with becoming a family grocer rather than a confectioner so he cut down the order and confined himself to selling bread from the same bakery. It was delicious bread with crackly brown crust where it had erupted above the tin and the customers loved its flavour. It was always sold out quickly but because it was not good for making sandwiches we had also to stock factory-made bread with crust that sagged when a knife was pressed against it and with a flavour that made best butter taste like margarine. We ate it at home only when there was nothing else.

Mr Josh was sitting with Father at the table one night sharing a supper of crusty bread and cheese. He was being entertained because he had come unexpectedly with the gift of a string-box specially designed and made by himself which, he claimed, would be more efficient than our present 'flimsy-flamsy'—a tin with a hole in it. Father thanked him with mild warmth. Mother eyed it with awe. It was a very capacious box—a ball of string would rattle around in it like a marble in a drawer—and it was made of solid teak weighing several pounds.

'That won't come to pieces in a hurry,' said Mr Josh, giving it an admiring slap. It was designed, he said, to be suspended from the ceiling and, eager to see his handiwork in operation, he had borrowed the step-ladder and attached the box to a convenient hook which to Mother's agitation was situated directly above the spot where she usually stood to serve. He inserted the ball of string, threaded it through the hole and pulled. The box swung threateningly but the string ran out as easily as line from a fishing rod.

'There you are, try it yourself,' Mr Josh invited Mother. She glanced apprehensively up at the heavy box.

'I'm afraid it might come down,' she said, pulling tentatively at the string.

'Well, there's one thing, if it does it won't be the box that'll suffer,' Mr Josh comforted her.

Satisfied that his gift was thoroughly appreciated he was now enjoying his supper. The cloth was spread on half the table. The other half was covered by the ironing sheet and the room was full of the smell of freshly ironed clothes. I was sitting on the step between the living room and the kitchen filling Father's bicycle lamp with pieces of carbide. Mr Josh munched steadily, but as he was taking his third slice of bread and butter from the plate he held it up. 'Isn't this the black man's bread?' he asked. I was so startled I knocked the lamp over. Father darted a repressive glance in my direction.

'Yes' he admitted reluctantly. 'Like it?'

'Aye,' said Mr Josh. 'It's good bread but dunna try sellin' it to the wife. She wouldn't have it in the house.'

I was outraged by Father's admission. They had let me eat and enjoy cakes and pies and bread made by a black man when I hadn't even known there was a black man in the town except on Friday nights when one came and sold herbal ointments at the open-air market. There were lascars who roamed the streets when their boats were in and there were Chinese whom I saw on Saturdays when I collected Father's stiff white collars from their laundry, but the lascars and the laundrymen were only yellow. Even so, I wouldn't have fancied food cooked by them. I retrieved the pieces of carbide and put them back in the lamp, promising myself I would do something really naughty to pay my parents back for their deceit.

Mr Josh spoke again with his mouth full of bread. 'Did you ever see his bakery?'

'I did,' responded Father. 'Clean as a new pin it was too. No sign of rats like some of the others I could mention.'

Mr Josh grunted. 'What's he like in himself?' he asked.

'He's not a bad chap at all,' said Father. 'A sad little bloke though; black as coal with tight curly grey hair and all dressed up in a clean white apron and white shoes with his arms white up to the elbows.'

I felt sick. If his arms were white up to the elbows where had the black gone? Had it come off into the bread? I was on the point of putting the question when Mr Josh spoke again.

'Where did you run into him?' he demanded. 'I've heard tell he never goes out at all.'

'He doesn't, except when it's dark,' Father told him. 'He realises people won't be so keen to buy his bread if they know he's a blackie so he never shows himself except for a quick dash to the pub just before closing time and then only in the winter. That's where I met him, at the Docks Inn. He bought me a pint.'

'Married a white woman, didn't he?' mused Mr Josh.

'Yes.' Father pushed away his plate and lit his pipe. 'She died when the child was born. The child died too. He still cries when he talks about it.'

Mother rested on the iron for a moment. 'Cries?' she asked incredulously. 'You don't expect a black man to be able to cry, somehow.'

Father accepted her remark with a wry glance. Mr Josh pursued his questioning.

'Who looks after the business if he doesn't show himself?'

'His sister-in-law, and her husband does the deliveries, so it's only white people seen around the place. He just does the baking and looks after the horse. He does look after the horse, too. The sister-in-law said he'd sleep in the stables with it if she'd let him.'

'They get on all right then, I mean his in-laws? Being white you'd think they might have been against him.'

'They told me they couldn't wish for a nicer man,' said

Father. 'And they're willing to look after him as long as he needs them.'

'That's a funny how-d'you-do,' opined Mr Josh. 'Proper funny that is.'

'I don't suppose the boat crews and the bargees would worry about him being black,' interpolated Mother.

'No,' Father agreed. 'But the way the docks are going down the nick there'll not be much more trade from that direction in the future. He'll have to sell elsewhere or go bust.' He got up, knocked out his pipe into the grate and pulled on his leggings and cape. 'It'll be a pity if he does,' he said. 'He's a hard worker.'

I had felt the stirrings of pity as I listened to the story of the black man, but I could not overcome my distaste.

As Father bent to kiss me goodbye I whispered passionately: 'I'll never eat his bread again.'

Father slapped my shoulders. 'Now you just stop playing at silly beggars, Chipcart,' he admonished me, and went out into the dark yard to get his bicycle. Mr Josh had cracked all his jokes and was ready to leave too. Mother carried the supper things through to the kitchen.

'If the black man's arms are white up to the elbows where has the black gone?' I demanded of Mr Josh.

His bright little eyes danced and he began to wheeze inwardly. 'Well, now,' he replied. 'When the black comes off in to the flour I daresay he just bakes brown bread with that batch.' He wheezed his way out.

Father was usually home and in bed snatching a few hours' sleep by the time I got up but the next morning he was sitting in front of the fire smoking when I came down to breakfast.

'Come here a minute, Chipcart,' he said. I went to him and he put an arm round me. 'Now I want you to promise me you'll never tell anyone that we buy our bread from a black man. It's very important. His bread's the best anybody could buy and his bakery's the cleanest I've seen so it shouldn't make any difference what colour he is. But some people are stupid and they wouldn't understand.' His voice was stern and I promised solemnly that I never would tell anyone—even accidentally. I never did. I never ate any of the baker's brown bread again, either.

6

The shop trade grew so quickly that Father was able to give up his job at the soap factory and devote himself entirely to the business. The lessons on attractive display in *The Practical Grocer* had been well learned and our shop window, high-lighted by a galaxy of clear, hand-painted price tickets, brought people from all over the town. Once they had set foot on the sawdusted floor they could choose from shelves stacked with packets, bottles, canisters and jars, all eye-catchingly arranged. The glass bottles of fruit were in themselves a spectacle of colour, ranging from the deep wine-red of loganberries to the bright red of raspberries; from the yellow-green of plump gooseberries to the old gold of spiced plums. White stoneware jars of jam stood one on top of the other like miniature Greek columns and on an adjoining shelf bottled sauces separated columns of tinned salmon. The egg racks were piled high in a mosaic of buff and white and brown; the tea shelves were tight with brightly coloured packets; the deep bread shelves bulged with golden crusts. Even the soap shelves down behind the counter were gay with 'Sunlight', 'Lifebuoy', 'New Pin' and 'Magical' soap packets; unwrapped brown and white windsor and long bars of a cream-coloured, blue-veined, scrubbing soap known as 'blue mottle' which was sold by the pound or half-pound and which had to be cut with a special soap knife. Along the front of the counter was affixed a frieze of glass-topped trays displaying different kinds of biscuits while in pride of place on the provision counter stood the handsome new scale flanked on one side by blocks of butter, lard and margarine and on the other by hams and assorted cuts of bacon. Whole cheeses made a bulwark between the window shelf and the counter. The shop soon attached to itself an aroma compounded of the smells of cooked meats and spice, fresh bread and cheese, piny sawdust and soap. Shop hours were full of noises: the chattering of customers; the patting and slapping of butter; the clang of weights on the scale; the prising open of biscuit tins; the sharpening of knives on steel, and the ring of the till bell. The row of knives was impressive. Two or three bacon-slicing knives, a thin-bladed boning knife and a special ham knife. There was a narrow-bladed, sharp-pointed cheese knife, for though cheese was usually cut with a wire the convention that customers should first sample the cheese they were buying was accepted as unquestioningly as

70

the convention that a diner should first sample the wine he orders. Delicately Father would push the point of the knife into the cheese and with a deft twist lever up a tiny morsel which he then held out on the end of the knife. The customer would take it, pop it into her mouth and pronounce judgment. Then Father usually dug a morsel for himself so that he could agree with her. I used to hear Mother telling customers how when she had first introduced Father to her parents as her prospective husband they had shaken their heads and told her solemnly to think again. He looked so frail, they said, she would most likely spend more of her life as a widow than as a wife. She used to weep at their warnings, but she married him just the same. 'And look at him now!' she used to say, and the customers laughed because after a few months of cheese tasting no one would have described Father as 'frail-looking'.

It was Father's ambition to build up a reputation for selling especially good bacon and cheese and probably because they were his own favourite foods he was particular in choosing the wholesaler he dealt with. I accompanied him once to the warehouse where rows of carcasses hung from rails as crowded as dresses in a wardrobe. Father wandered round, followed like a lackey by the foreman in a grease-smeared overall who noted Father's comments as he chose or rejected sides. Father looked first for good curing and firm texture, then for leanness and flavour and seemed able to tell whether or not the bacon was likely to be too salty just by smelling it. When he had finished I thought I saw him tip the foreman. As an additional insurance of his being sent good bacon, Father made a great fuss of the firm's traveller, who visited the shop each week to solicit orders. Invariably there was a cup of tea and a slice of Mother's johnny cake for the traveller when he came and in return he assured Father that he personally inspected every side that was sent to us. Whether or not there was any truth in his assurance I do not know, but though people might get all the rest of of their goods from their local grocer, if they could manage it they came, sometimes by pony and trap, sometimes on three-wheeler bicycles, sometimes by bus, to buy their bacon at our shop.

The railway wagon used to bring the bacon, four sides at a time, each side wrapped in coarse hessian to protect it from the dust and dirt of the journey. The wagon signalled its arrival with a plodding of heavy hooves, a shout from the driver, a grinding of wheels, a snort from the horse as the reins pulled him to a halt. If I was at hand I had to scurry to open the back door and the storeroom door and see that the passageway was free from impediment. Sides of bacon are heavy and cumbersome and the unloading was always done with a rush, not because the driver was impatient to get away, but because Sam, the great dun-coloured carthorse whose yellow whiskers curled aristocratically out of his nostrils, always waited deliberately until he was outside our shop before indulging in his morning piddle. At least Father always swore it was deliberate and he started to fret as soon as he heard the first clip-clop of Sam's hooves but no matter how much he hurried and exhorted the work was rarely completed in time for that blessed horse to perform elsewhere. Inevitably the great hissing stream of urine gushed lengthily and frothily on to the road directly in front of the shop to run down the gutter beside the pavement. Passers-by and potential customers would hurriedly cross to the other side of the road to avoid being splashed and for a time the smell drifting in through the open door overpowered the customary aroma of the shop.

The sides of bacon were left in the storeroom until the shop was closed for the evening at seven o'clock, when they were unwrapped and laid one at a time on a trestle table in the yard in readiness for washing. Most grocers were content to give the bacon a sketchy wipe down with a damp cloth which meant that it could be cut straight away without waiting for it to dry but Father insisted on washing every bit of bacon that was delivered and after I had seen him shaking out the dust from the hessian wrappings I was glad he did. I used to be given a clean dry cloth and when Father had finished swabbing hot water over the bacon, cleaning carefully under the curled edges and between the rib bones my job was to mop it as dry as possible. When he was satisfied that the job was done well Father took his sharpest knife and pared off small pieces of rind which bore the blue stamp branding it as 'Swedish', which had been explained to me as being necessary because our customers believed they were buying 'Danish' bacon and he was afraid one or two of them might be astute enough to notice that 'Danish' bacon bore red stamp marks. I was shocked at first to discover that Father, who punished me for cheating or telling lies, should be capable of doing so himself, but I soon grew accustomed to such deceptions as being part of normal shopkeeping practice. When Father handed me a damp cloth and a packet of 'Vim' and instructed me to rub the 'Irish' stamp off a consignment of eggs so that they could be sold as 'Fresh' my only reaction was fear that Father might be found out and put in prison.

Once the brand marks had been removed from the bacon it was powdered all over with a mixture of herbs and spices compounded by Mother; this was supposed to deter flies while the sides hung to dry in a large gauze safe which ran nearly the whole length of the backyard. With the bacon disposed of for the time being, the trestle table had to be scrubbed and dismantled; the yard swilled down with strong soda water and scrubbed with a stiff broom, by which time it was most likely to be coming up to ten o'clock. If he was lucky Father might just have time to nip down to the pub for a quick drink, for despite having in his youth 'signed the pledge' at the Wesleyan chapel, once the shop was opened

Father seemed to find that a glass of Guinness was not only good for him but for the business.

·   ·   ·   ·   ·

The Cheshire cheese we sold in the shop came direct from the farm and every so often Father hitched a lift with Uncle Dick, who had now become interested in pork butchering, when he drove out to the farms in his pony and trap to buy piglets. I was still in awe of Uncle Dick but not enough to overcome my delight in being taken for long drives through fragrant country lanes, every tippety-tap of the pony's feet bringing me nearer to the farmyards with their inevitable ponds and ducks and squealing pigs and curious hens. With the first day of the school holidays I started to estimate or question the likely date of the next cheese buying and pleaded with Father to ask Uncle Dick if I might accompany them. The answer being in the affirmative I was jigging about on the pavement outside the shop for at least half an hour before Uncle Dick was due. The trap turned into the street drawn by Bandage the pony—so called because he had a broad band of white round his tummy like a frayed rag—and Father got in beside Uncle Dick. I climbed up behind them and tucked myself in to the deep straw that littered the floor. The strawed floor was not meant for my comfort but for bedding down the piglets which Uncle Dick expected to buy and with whom I should have to share the straw on the return journey. Sometimes if the pigs were noisy or restless my discomfort would be so great that I'd think to myself I wouldn't ask to be taken again, for no matter how uncomfortable I was I did not dare make a whimper of protest in case Uncle Dick heard. The big horse whip reared itself so menacingly within reach of his right hand and I had no doubt he would use it on me if I displeased him. I used to stare at his large unyielding back and think about the poor orphaned children who had once been taken in the trap for their first glimpse of the country. The orphans, three little boys, were protégées of some menial of the chapel on whom Aunty Rye wished to bestow a more magnànimous reward than her usual gift of a cold rice pudding so it was at her instigation they were commanded to take an afternoon's airing with Uncle Dick. Having been repeatedly enjoined that in return for such beneficence they must sit perfectly still throughout the whole journey and not utter a sound, the mouselike little boys had burrowed into the straw hardly daring to lift a hand in response to the goodbye waves of their guardian. The silence had lasted until the trap had left the town and was proceeding along a deserted country lane when a small voice piped up tremulously: 'Oh, please, sir . . .'

Without turning his head Uncle Dick had sternly rebuked him. 'Quiet there!' he commanded and drove on.

'But please, sir,' another voice piped up more urgently after they had travelled a while longer.

'Less noise from you children or you'll be put out of the trap and have to walk back,' rasped Uncle Dick again without turning his head. They had covered a good distance before a third voice was courageous enough to try and attract his attention.

'Please, sir, please . . .' The plea ended with a sob. Uncle Dick was outraged. It was bad enough having disobedient children in his trap—but blubbering children! He reined in Bandage and turned round ready to quell the three orphans with savage threats. But there were only two little figures in the straw and the door of the trap was swinging open. 'Please, sir,' they sobbed piteously, 'our Willy fell out a long way back.'

Uncle Dick had turned the trap and driven back immediately, of course, but they had to go nearly two miles before they found Willy lying in the road with both his legs broken.

It was nearly always the same farm we visited to buy both

pigs and cheese and immediately we arrived Father and Uncle Dick, escorted by the farmer, went off in the direction of the pigsties: I was told to go and pull a handful of hay for the pony and then to go and pick a bunch of flowers for my mother from the overcrowded garden at the side of the house. When Father came back I was waiting ready, for I wouldn't have missed the cheese buying for anything. The farmer led the way through the kitchen, down two or three steps and pushed open a heavy arched door. The cheese room was dim and cool and musty smelling with a thick slate shelf round the walls on which stood a phalanx of cheeses tightly bound in white cloth and ranged in order of maturity so that the newest made ones were immediately to the left of the door and the ripest ones to the right. Father indicated a cheese somewhere about the centre of the phalanx and the farmer deftly pushed in the long cheese borer, which was rather like an over-long apple corer. When it was withdrawn it was full of cheese and we each scraped a little out with a finger and popped it into our mouths.

'A little bit on the sharp side for my customers,' Father said. 'What do you think, Chipcart?'

I wrinkled my nose. It was much too sharp for me.

The farmer plunged his borer into another cheese a little to the left of the first one. 'This should be milder,' he said.

'A bit on the crumbly side, this one,' Father observed when a few bits dropped from his fingers. 'I'd lose too much in the cutting.'

'There's been a mouse at this one.' Uncle Dick rapped a cheese with his knuckles.

'Then it'll be a good cheese right enough,' responded the farmer with a wink. 'They say it's always the best cheese the mouse goes for. Look now! See for yourself. There's not one of the others touched.'

When we had tasted it we agreed with the mouse.

'We'll have that one for a start,' Father said. 'But I'll need a bob knocking off it for the mouse nibble.' The farmer grunted assent and marked the cheese with a pencil.

They moved on. By this time I had tasted enough cheese and had turned my attention to the big iron cheese press which stood in the centre of the stone floor.

'Dunna you squash yourself in that or us'll have to wrap you up in cheese cloth and pack you off to market,' teased the farmer. 'And what label would we put on you, now? "Squashed Cheshire"? Or "Pressed Cream"?'

Father flicked me a grin. '"Ripe Gorgonzola," I'd think,' he said, which made me blush because I knew Gorgonzola cheese smelled disgustingly.

When sufficient cheese had been ordered we came out from the gloom of the cheese room into the big airy farm kitchen.

'I think the missus has a drop of buttermilk if you'd care for a sup,' said the farmer, and went outside to call his wife. Father and Uncle Dick always looked forward to their drink of buttermilk, but despite coaxing and the promise that drinking it would make my hair curl and my cheeks rosy I could not bring myself to touch it. The farmer returned, followed by his wife, who bore an enormous jug that looked about the size of the ewer which stood on the washstand in my bedroom. The farmer's wife was very pretty: she had blue eyes and black curly hair and a tomato red face with more black curly hair on her upper lip and round her chin which I found almost too fascinating to take my eyes away from. I supposed she must have drunk an awful lot of buttermilk. She reached up to the dresser and took down four mugs and while I watched anxiously as she filled three of them with buttermilk I was willing her not to forget that I didn't like it. I need not have worried; she took the fourth mug out to the dairy and brought it back full of fresh milk for me. She sawed away at the crust of a fresh-baked loaf and spread the dishevelled slices with home-made butter while her husband opened a cupboard and brought out a huge wedge of crocus-yellow cheese.

'This is where the good ones go,' said Father slyly and the farmer's wife tittered.

'And can you blame me with the price I get for them?' responded the farmer.

Father and Uncle Dick drew up chairs to the white wood table and tucked into bread and cheese. I was only cake hungry so I sat staring at the plate of seed cake until I was offered a piece.

'Has the young miss finished?' the farmer asked, wiping a hand across his mouth.

I had finished what I had but I was hoping for another piece of seed cake so I looked at Father.

'Yes, she has,' he said treacherously. 'She'll not eat her tea when she gets home if she has any more now.'

'Well then, I've something to show her,' said the farmer. 'You come this way, young miss.'

I followed him back through the kitchen, down the steps and past the cheese room along a narrow, windowless passage. There was another arched doorway at the end of the passage just like the one into the cheese room. The farmer lifted the latch and kicked the door open.

'Mind the steps, now,' he warned. 'Just four of them there is, so count them as you go.' I counted four and found myself in a room about a quarter the size of the cheese room and about twice as dim.

'This is the apple room,' the farmer explained. I looked around. Racks lined the walls but though there was a lingering apple smell there were no apples to be seen, only a large heap of rubble on the floor.

'See that now.' The farmer was pointing to a low archway in the wall opposite the door. Below it was a large hole from which the rubble had obviously been excavated. 'That hole there's the beginning of a secret passage if I'm not mistaken,' he said.

I stared in incredulous wonder, unable to speak for excitement. I knew the farmhouse was supposed to be very old. I knew that it's little arched doorways were more like the doors of crypts and vestries in church than like house doors but it was such a busy, homely place that I had never suspected it harboured anything more secretive than spiders in the attics and mice in the cellars. The farmer took a pickaxe from the mound of rubble and chipped at the hole. There was a skittering of more rubble.

I found my voice at last. 'A secret passage?' I gasped.

'That's what I reckon. This old house used to be a monastery once upon a time and there's what they call priest-holes up in the attics but they're not like this one. No, you just watch this.' He lit a candle and held it near the hole. The flame bent to the draught. The farmer shielded it with his hand and the flame burned straight again. He moved his hand and the flame bent again. 'That means there's air coming in there from somewhere and my bet is it's a secret passage.'

'Where to?' I asked

'That I dunno,' he replied. 'But there's always been a belief round here that there was a passage between this place and the old hall back yonder so maybe this is it.'

'Oh, do please let's go on digging,' I begged. 'I'll help.'

The farmer chuckled. 'And what'll Master Dick and your father say to that? No, young missy, you must get back home and I must get to my cows but next time you're over maybe I'll have a bit more to show you.'

Reluctantly I followed him back to the kitchen where Father and Uncle Dick were standing by the door watching the cows being brought up for milking.

'Time to go, Chipcart,' said Father.

The farmer's wife bent down and whispered in my ear. I

nodded and made for the well-worn path that skirted the privet hedge round the garden and led to a small brick shed. I was familiar with the brick shed now but the first time I had visited the farm's earth closet I had been perplexed at being confronted with three identical holes in the long wooden seat, each with its own wooden lid. I had worked out that as the farmer's family comprised father, mother and son the three holes must be a father hole, a mother hole and a son hole, and though I was shocked at the idea of their all using the lavatory together I realised how glad I should be of companionship if I'd had to go so far from the house on a dark winter's night. But the question was, which hole I should use? I imagined the family grumbling, like the three bears, 'Who's been using my hole?' and so fearful was I of using the wrong one that I decided to risk having an accident on the way home. After all, I could always blame it on the pigs.

Father and Uncle Dick were waiting beside the trap when I got back and I was stuffed in beside two squirming sacks with a piglet's head protruding from each. The farmer's wife handed up my bunch of flowers which she had added to while I was at the brick house so that instead of the handful I had picked my arms were full of a confusion of colour and fragrance. I held them resolutely close to my face, warding off the pig smell.

The next time I visited the farm the secret passage had been excavated far enough for me to take three big paces into it. The farmer showed me a ring he had unearthed in the rubble, but it didn't look anything like secret treasure, the metal being greeny and the stone, when the farmer scratched at it with a thumbnail, an opaque blue. I thought it a very shabby ring compared with the glittery one I had got from a Christmas cracker.

'I'll get this cleaned up and then you can have it for a keepsake,' the farmer promised. 'It's not much of a ring but it'll be nice for you to have.' He put it in his pocket. 'I'll have it ready for you next time you come,' he said. 'And by then maybe I'll have found where this passage is going to lead.'

But there never was a next time. The farmer died of a stroke soon afterwards and the farm was sold. The new owner, who had no interest in secret passages, only complained of the draught in the apple room and had the hole blocked up again as far as the archway. As for the blue stone ring I never heard what happened to that. Father, who had also been shown it and dismissed it like the farmer as 'not much of a ring', said it had probably been thrown out with the rest of the rubbish.

The death of the kind old farmer made me sad and the abrupt end to what I had dreamed of as being a great adventure was an aching disappointment. Father was disappointed too: the new farmer didn't even make good cheese.

7

Fridays and Saturdays were the busiest days in the shop and though during the rest of the week the regulation closing time was seven o'clock on Friday nights, it was permitted to stay open until eight and on Saturdays nine o'clock. The closing times had to be strictly observed and the shopkeeper who supplied goods even two minutes after the statutory hour ran the risk of being caught by an indefatigable lurker of an inspector and brought up before the local court. There were, of course, anomalies: it was illegal for a grocer to supply a tin of milk after hours to feed a starving baby but not for him to supply the father with cigarettes. Similarly he must not supply oatmeal for an invalid's gruel though he was perfectly at liberty to supply sweets for the theatregoer.

The initial fine for such an offence was negligible but the stigma both for shopkeeper and customer was great; for the shopkeeper because he was a member of a trading association which deplored such furtive practices and for the customer because her name would appear in the paper and she would be branded as improvident. When a late customer came knocking at our shop door we had to tell her through the letter-box to go round to the back where she would be admitted only after a look round to ensure the inspector was nowhere in the vicinity. She might want 'a candle to see the children to bed' or 'an egg for my husband's breakfast'. Whatever it was had to be small enough to be slipped into a pocket and it was supplied with the proviso that she went home along the back alley and the instruction that if the inspector stopped her—as he had every right to do—she was to say the goods had been ordered and paid for earlier and she was only collecting them. Sometimes a customer might be desperate for bread which was too bulky to be disguised and the ruse then was to take a slice off a loaf so that the inspector could be assured it was only borrowed bread from our larder.

There was one of our customers who was almost a regular night visitor and though she or her children were in the shop half a dozen times a day there was always something she desperately needed after closing time. She was Irish, feckless, improvident and irrepressibly jovial and though she constantly had an outstanding balance of around twenty pounds which she was reluctantly paying off at a shilling a week she was our most irresistible customer. Father could tease her as he teased a child and she laughed uproariously; he could rebuke her in the same way and she had forgotten it within seconds. Her husband had a steady job but winter or sweltering summer 'Irish's' uncorseted bulk was bundled into an old tweed coat that looked as if it had been left over from a jumble sale. Save for a frying pan she had no pots or pans in the house, a fact we discovered when she admitted that for years she had yearned for mashed potatoes but as the Gas Company had supplied only a roasting tin with the cooker they always had to have their potatoes roasted. Her home was scrupulously clean yet they hadn't enough chairs for the family of four to sit down at one time. They had no clock so they had to rely on instinct corroborated by factory sirens and school bells for their time keeping which might have accounted for her habitual late appearances at the shop. Sometimes if she had squandered the week's money 'Irish' wouldn't come near the shop for days and Father would go to see what she intended to do about paying her bill. Always he came back shaking his head and laughing over the comedy he had witnessed. On one occasion one of the children had opened the door and told him, 'Mammy isn't in.' Father knew she was and said he would go inside and wait, which he did, noticing that the children glanced anxiously every now and then at the door of the coal-hole. He went over and opened it and there was 'Irish' crouched on the heap of coal trying not to make a sound.

'What did she say?' asked Mother.

' "Good afternoon",' Father told her.

Mother was flabbergasted. 'Is that all?'

'It was all at first,' said Father, 'and it took my breath away a bit, but when I told her I was glad to find she was in after all she said, "I was just looking to see if I could pay my bill with coal this week, seeing I have no money".'

On another occasion Father resolved to go to the house when 'Irish's' husband, a quiet, hardworking man, was at home. Suspecting that 'Irish' concealed from him the extent of her debts he felt that an interview with the husband might improve the situation. The door was again opened by one of the children and he was invited inside where he found 'Irish' lying on a length of flowery cotton on the kitchen floor while her husband cut round her shape for a nightdress. Father gave up. He said he couldn't talk seriously under the circumstances.

Despite 'Irish's' affinity with debts she regularly included all kinds of luxuries in her weekly order. Almost as regularly Father crossed them off and when the boxes of chocolates or tinned lobster failed to arrive she accepted the reproof with plaintive good humour. If she desired some particular luxury very much she came to the shop to plead with Father and when he proved resolute she would, still with a laugh, delve into her pocket, produce the cash to pay for it and depart triumphantly. Once when she had ordered a number of articles which Father knew would only be added to her debit balance he not only crossed them off the list but told 'Irish' sharply that she must not ask for luxuries she could not pay for. The expression on her face was like that of a bereft child.

'But I must have them. My brother and his wife are coming over for the day on Sunday and I've got to give them something nice.'

'If you need the things that badly you can find the money for them,' Father told her sternly. 'I've got my own relatives to feed on Sunday and I can't afford to feed yours.'

'But I haven't got the money, honest.'

'You find the money to take the family to the pictures four times a week,' countered Father. We had two picture houses in our town and the picture was changed twice weekly. 'Irish' and her family never missed a picture and though they sat in what was known locally as the 'Bug Rack', which cost fourpence for adults and twopence for children, four shillings a week was far more than most people could afford to spend on entertainment.

'Irish' looked baffled. 'But we can't miss the serials!' she wailed. 'We'd never sleep at night if we didn't know what was happening to the "Black Phantom".' She began to plead. 'You can't let me down, not with my relatives coming. I've got to have something nice for them to eat and people expects fruit salad and cream on Sundays.' Her voice trailed off as she saw Father's mouth tighten purposefully.

'I'll let you have the ingredients to bake a cake and a pound of cooking apples,' he offered. 'It won't make your bill so big.'

Irish's' guffaws of laughter nearly rattled the tins off the shelves. 'Me? Make a cake? I've never done such a thing in my life and I wouldn't know how,' she burst out. 'You might as well offer me a packet of bird seed to feed them on.'

Her laughter died down and her expression became a little tense. 'Aren't you going to let me have them?' she wheedled. 'Just this once?'

The game was always played this way and Father was expecting her to produce the money eventually, but 'Irish' turned towards the shop door. 'Oh, well, the best thing I can do is go home and put my head in the gas oven,' she said sadly, and bundled herself out.

'She'll be back,' said Father confidently and back she was less than an hour later, her fat face crumpled with smiles. She slapped the money down on the counter.

'Here you are,' she said, with a faint attempt at lugubriousness.

'I thought you'd find it if you looked hard enough,' said Father as he handed her the goods.

'I found it at the pawn shop,' she confided roguishly. 'I pledged Pat's jacket and that good belt with brass pictures on it he has for keeping up his trousers.'

Father laughed. 'And what's he going to keep his trousers up with till he gets it back again?' he asked.

'Irish' caught her bottom lip between her teeth. 'I'm glad you reminded me,' she said. 'Can you spare me a couple of yards of string?'

. . . . .

It was fortunate that the majority of our customers were not like 'Irish' or Father would have been bankrupt within a few weeks. There were other debtors, of course, but while 'Irish' rollicked into debt the rest slid into it gradually. Allowing ten shillings for the weekly grocery bill they'd find it came to eleven or twelve and so the extra shillings would have to be added to a 'balance' that increased weekly. Some appeared indifferent, believing no doubt that debit balances vanished if ignored. Others fretted and cut their orders down to bare necessities until the bill was paid, and it was one of these customers, Mrs Dainty, who for a time worried my parents a great deal. Mrs Dainty was a small woman with a sweet face and a jittery manner and when she had first brought her custom to us her husband, who was much older than she, had a good job as manager of one of the local stores. Though she was always careful with money she never had to skimp either on quantity or quality of the food for the family which comprised herself, her husband and their most attractive and beautifully brought-up little boy. His name was Billy; he had wide blue eyes, fair curly hair and a gentle inquisitiveness of manner which enchanted everyone who came into contact with him. With Father he was a great favourite, being allowed to come behind the counter and explore the shelves; lifted up to put weights on the scales and to open and close the till so that the bell would ring.

One day the husband had an accident at work which crippled him and as the owners of the store denied liability a long battle had to be fought to gain compensation. At first they lived on their small savings but when these had gone Mrs Dainty went out charring; dug the garden and grew vegetables to sell; took in dressmaking and minded other people's children—anything in fact to earn a little money to keep them alive. As the weeks and months went by Father noticed the Dainty order for groceries growing less and less each week, though the bill was always paid. He saw that Billy was outgrowing his clothes despite lengthenings and widenings, and that there were no new ones replacing them. He remarked to Mother on how thin and strained Mrs Dainty herself was becoming. When the weekly order had decreased to only five items Father resolved to do something about it. 'We can't let her starve herself to death,' he told Mother.

'I don't know how you're going to approach her, though,' said Mother.

'I know what to do,' said Father. I was out of sight stacking cigarette cartons under the counter next time Mrs Dainty came into the shop and as Father seemed to have forgotten I was there I was able to hear every word that passed.

When Mrs Dainty handed in her order he glanced at it and continued to hold the slip of paper in his hand.

'Mrs Dainty,' he challenged her, and his voice was abnormally crisp. 'Are you dissatisfied with the service or the goods we're sending you?'

'Oh, no,' she denied instantly. 'You mustn't think that.'

'I cannot help thinking it when I see how little you buy from us nowadays. Your order used to be three and four times as big.' Mrs Dainty said nothing and Father went on. 'Of course, if you prefer to buy your groceries elsewhere I must accept it but I've always tried to do my best for you and I should like to know the reason for your leaving us.'

Mrs Dainty started to sob and the whole story came out. With an invalid husband and a child she could not earn enough money to support the three of them so she and her husband had decided they could live on bread and a scrape of margarine for their meals; the small amount of butter she ordered was used only for Billy, as were the few other items. So long as they could keep the child well fed, she said, they didn't mind.

Father's voice became gentle. 'How long since you've eaten a cooked meal?' he asked her.

Mrs Dainty shook her bowed head. She didn't know.

'I think we'll add a few things to your list then, shall we?' he said, and taking a pencil increased the quantity of butter, added bacon and cheese and tea.

'I can't pay for them,' wailed Mrs Dainty. 'Not at any rate till we get some compensation money.'

'I'll wait till then,' Father told her firmly.

'It might be a year or more,' she objected feebly.

'I'll wait,' said Father, and made her promise that she would take a regular order for all the things she needed and not worry about payment until she had the money.

Mother, who had purposely kept out of the way during the interview, came into the shop as soon as Mrs Dainty had gone. She looked at Father enquiringly and he told her of Mrs Dainty's confession and promise.

'I'm glad to hear it.' said Mother with relief.

'I'm glad to do it,' said Father. 'But she's lucky she's not dealing with one of the multiple shops. I don't see them being willing to supply groceries on a promise. Not for as long as this is likely to be.'

'I hope it's not too long,' said Mother. 'It's going to mount up to a lot of money.'

Father almost glared at her. 'She'll pay sometime,' he affirmed. 'I've no doubt of that.' He was right. The day the compensation came through Mrs Dainty was the first customer in the shop, asking for her bill right up to date and happily signing a cheque.

8

Although the shop door was firmly closed at seven o'clock and the window blind lowered Father usually worked on until half past nine weighing and packaging goods to replenish the shelves. Except for branded teas, ready-packeted goods were virtually unavailable and though *The Practical Grocer* noted that a New York store was devoting itself entirely to the sale of such goods the writer thought the introduction of ready-made bags was in itself a great stride forward. Until then the grocer had not only to weigh out the goods but make his bags also. We still made bags for pounds of sugar and bulk teas by rolling a cone of paper, twisting it at the bottom and tucking in the top flaps but everything else went into prepared bags.

There were so many goods which had to be weighed out: 2 lb sugar, butter, lard, margarine, peas, cocoa, flour, rice, dried fruits, soap flakes, starch, candles, and it saved time when the shop was full of customers if these things could be reached already packed from a shelf. The shop demanded the sacrifice of all Father's leisure save for the twenty minutes or so he spent down at the pub. Half-closing days were devoted to window-dressing, Sundays to book-keeping, and even I had my set tasks when I was not at school. On Saturdays when I was not running messages I was likely to be cleaning dried fruit, which entailed rubbing the fruit around in a large sieve, breaking up the tight sticky lumps and picking out the stalks and pieces of straw which looked suspiciously like floor-sweepings. On Sunday mornings I had the monotonous job of turning the handle of the grindstone while Father sharpened all the knives.

In the evenings I often worked beside Father until it was my bedtime, filling bags of sugar ready for him to weigh, counting out candles and long slim tapers ready for him to wrap and string. We sold two kinds of candles, 'carriage' and 'household', and two kinds of tapers, plain white ones at fourpence a pound and coloured ones at sixpence. If they could afford them people liked to buy the coloured ones because they looked so pretty when stood in an ornament on the mantelpiece.

They were pleasant times, these hours spent with Father, almost as good as the evenings we used to spend together before his night-shift job at the factory and the shop put an end to them. Then we had made moving pictures with cardboard shapes and a candle and a cloth draped over a stool, or Father had developed camera plates in the darkened kitchen while I had agitated the prints in a bowl of hypo. Now, though it was working evenings, we still had fun. Father talked of his childhood and of his own strict upbringing. Grandfather, it seemed, had been a stern but gentle disciplinarian and though he rarely thrashed his sons his means of punishing them was more than effective. I heard how Father and his brother had been sauntering home from school one afternoon, watching the road-sweeper at work. The old man had swept along the gutter leaving the dirt in piles so that he could work back and collect it with his barrow which he had left at the corner. The two boys had waited until the sweeper's back was turned and then kicked each pile of dirt into the roadway. Unfortunately, unknown to them Grandfather had been watching and when they decided it was time to run away they headed straight for the spot where he stood waiting. He marched them back to the road-sweeper, made them apologise, and instructing the man to hand over his brush and shovel and barrow to the two boys made them work along the street, sweeping up all the dirt and loading it into the barrow. Father said they were so ashamed it was a long time before they even dared walk along that street again.

Another time they had not only trespassed in a farmer's field but had stolen one of the turnips and as their escapade had made them late getting home for their tea they had taken the turnip as a peace offering, saying that the farmer had given it to them. Grandfather had seemed impressed and asked if they had remembered to thank the farmer for his gift. The boys said they had.

'Just exactly what did you say?' asked Grandfather. The boys blushed and weren't sure so, without any tea and carrying the turnip, they were marched back to the farm where they were confronted by the farmer, who, of course, denied that they had come by the turnip legitimately. Grandfather had insisted they not only go back to the field but replace the turnip in the spot from which they had lifted it. When they eventually reached home again they were sent to bed without tea or supper. 'We wouldn't have pinched a stray feather from a hen run after that,' Father said.

Sometimes we talked about the customers at the shop and some of the funny things they said: the girl who came every week for 'a pound of best dangerous bacon' when she meant 'Danish'; the woman who always asked for her bacon to be 'cut with a hammy knife'; the lounger on the dole who came in regularly to ask for cigarettes in a scraped voice which, prodding at his Adam's apple, he diagnosed as 'enlarge-itis', and the harassed young mother of a child wailing with hunger who dashed in on her way to catch a bus.

'Didn't you have time to give him his dinner before you came out?' Mother asked.

'I didn't have time to give him nothing but a piece of cheese and a smacked bottom,' retorted the mother as she dashed out again.

Father often made songs up about our customers, or I believed he had made them up, and we sang them together, sharing the secret opportunity to be disrespectful. One was about a Mrs Moy who Father thought was the ugliest woman he had ever seen and it went:

'Oh, she was a rummy old guy,
She had a double-barrelled squint in her eye,
And an india-rubber lip like the rudder of a ship,
And a mouth like a crack in a pie.'

Another was about a Mrs Vigger who happened to be very small:

'There was a Mrs Vigger and she couldn't grow no bigger,

So they put her in a wild beast show.
She tumbled through the window and she broke her
   little finger,
And she couldn't play the old banjo.'

I was sometimes inclined to sulk at having to give up so many of my Saturdays to the shop, especially when it was dried-fruit cleaning, but often I preferred working to playing with the children of the neighbourhood. Cora had proved a dull companion, becoming animated only when there was a death and a funeral in the neighbourhood or a horse bolted or some similar calamity. The rest of the time she liked to pry on the behaviour of the locals while she pushed someone's baby around in a pram. The other girls were rough-mannered and rough-voiced. They wore tattered boots and stockings with big holes in them and they wandered about the streets eating 'jam butties'; my parents deplored my being seen in their company. I hadn't seen Fran for a long time. When we had moved to the shop I was taken away from the Primary School we had both attended and sent to the big Council School not far from the house where, after a test, I had been put in a class with girls much older than myself. I hated every minute I was at that school; most of the pupils were noisy and vulgar; most of the teachers tense and shrill-voiced, reinforcing their instructions with displays of temper and canings. My 'quarter to nine' pains assailed me more frequently and when I was released at four o'clock I returned home as directly as a ball on a piece of elastic instead of the happy dawdling I'd known with Fran. When I reached home I'd have to have my hair scrutinised for lice and combed with a fine-toothed comb.

It was a wonderful surprise one Friday evening when I peeped into the shop to see Fran's mother there and, on opening the door wider, to perceive Fran standing beside her. I sidled round to the front of the counter and we greeted each other with shy eagerness. At first we didn't seem to know what to say to each other but Fran showed me the new chain purse she had been given for a birthday present and I made her show it to Mother because I wanted one for my birthday.

Fran's mother was collecting quite a pile of goods on the counter and my parents were being very attentive to her, so Fran and I turned to inspect the big stack of biscuit tins near the door.

'Can you just come and help yourself to biscuits whenever you feel like it?' whispered Fran.

'Not always,' I admitted, with a quick glance at my parents, because I knew my answer should truthfully have been 'not ever'.

Fran pulled at her mother's coat, demanding attention. 'Can we buy some biscuits?'

'Yes, very well,' replied her mother tolerantly. 'We'll have a pound of mixed biscuits, please.'

Father pulled a bag from the strung bundle and started to come round to the front of the counter.

'Please,' piped up Fran. 'Can I choose them and Chipcart weigh them?'

Father looked dubious for a second, but nodded and handed the bag to me. It was a rapturous few minutes for me as I opened tins and showed Fran all my favourites, dropped a few of each into the bag and put them on the scale. I'd been allowed to weigh out things like soap flakes and starch that didn't matter much how disreputable the bag looked when I'd finished but this was the first time I had ever been allowed to really serve anyone while the shop was open. I grew bold.

'Please may Fran and I have a chocolate biscuit each now?' I asked.

Father said yes but at the same time flicked me a look that let me know I was going to be told off later. I didn't mind. It was worth it to be munching and sharing with Fran again.

Fran asked, 'Can you come with me to the third landing tomorrow?'

Tomorrow was a Saturday and I longed to be able to go with her but Mother had made no pretence of her relief when she thought the friendship between me and Fran had been severed and I was worried that she might not allow a resumption. I glanced first at Mother and then at Father. They were packing goods into the basket for Fran's mother and were all attention and affability. I heard Fran's mother promising to place a regular order and judged this to be the right moment.

I nudged Fran. 'You ask,' I whispered.

Fran spoke up. 'Please can Chipcart come with me to the third landing tomorrow for a picnic?'

I saw that they were taken aback but I was sure they wouldn't dare refuse and perhaps risk losing a customer.

'Yes, very well,' said Father, and this time he flicked a glance at Mother which I knew meant 'We'll talk this over later'.

Fran and I turned to each other with ecstatic smiles.

'I'll call for you at half past one,' Fran promised. 'And we'll get some dandelion and nettle pop.'

'I'll be ready,' I assured her.

. . . . .

It was a lovely sunny afternoon and I was waiting eagerly for Fran with my pack of sandwiches wrapped in an old towel. I had half suspected my parents would raise some objection at the last minute to my going but Mother had cut my sandwiches without a murmur and popped in two slices of cake, one of which, though she couldn't bring herself to say so, I knew was for Fran. As soon as Fran arrived we dashed off to buy our pop from Mrs Brown who made dandelion and nettle pop (some called it 'beer' but being a

Wesleyan I had to call it 'pop') in the big wash boiler in her shed and sold it to anyone who rattled at her backyard door. Fran and I jiggled the latch until Mrs Brown appeared. She was a shiningly clean woman, wearing clogs and a sack apron and a man's cap and her face and arms were as red and scrubbed-looking as the bricks of her backyard. We offered her our pennies and in return she handed us two big bottles of pop, their corks securely tied down with string.

'Carry 'em careful and when you brings empty bottle back you'll get 'apenny back for 'em,' she told us in her clogs-and-sack-apron voice. 'An' dun forget the corks!' she screamed after us.

It was a three-mile walk to the third landing, which was a muddy creek along the ship canal, sometimes known as 'Tim Pop's Gutter', and on sunny Saturdays in summer it was a favourite place for families to picnic. For many it was the nearest they ever got to the seaside and they trudged across the fields, ignoring the faded 'Danger' and 'Trespassers will be prosecuted' signs, so that the children could paddle or fish for crabs with a fish head on the end of a piece of string while the parents sat on the bank and watched the ships go by and everyone acquired a vestige of sun-tan. The 'Danger' notice was not irrelevant since the shallow water stretched only for about six yards before it plunged steeply to the full depth of the canal, but children were cautioned not to paddle beyond the point where the water came to up their knees and there were always plenty of adults to administer a sharp rebuke to any child who might behave foolishly.

Fran and I took off our shoes and socks immediately we arrived and pulling our knickers up over our skirts like all the other girls we crept into the water until it reached our ankles. Someone shouted 'Here's a boat!' and we stood waiting to scream and 'jump the waves' as the wash came rolling in. The bigger the boat that passed the bigger was the wash and the louder the screams and there was a succession of boats passing that day.

As soon as we observed the first picnickers unpacking their food Fran and I, realising how hungry we were, climbed on to the sun-warmed grass of the bank where we ate and drank and were chased by three boys brandishing crabs and threatening to put them down the backs of our dresses if they caught us. Two of the boys we knew would carry out their threat, but the third, Bobbie Jones, was a gentle, quiet boy and we knew we were safe from him; all the same he was allowed to share with the other two some of our sandwiches and pop as a bribe for not molesting us. We paddled again and jumped more waves, but when we heard mothers calling their elder children from the water and saw toddlers being strapped into push chairs we knew it was time for us to go and we retrieved our towels and the precious pop bottles and started for home.

Fran said, 'D'you think you'll be able to come again next Saturday?'

'I don't know if my parents will let me,' I admitted.

'Make them let you,' said Fran imperiously.

'I can't,' I protested.

'Why not?' she argued. 'I made my mother come and buy at your shop and I'm going to make her come every week.'

I felt myself smiling inside. 'I expect I'll be able to come then,' I said.

But we never did go again.

It was Cora, the lover of calamity, who brought us the news on Sunday morning that Bobbie Jones was missing and that the police were dragging the canal at the third landing. It was on Tuesday evening that we saw his body being carried home. Fran and I, feeling that the tragedy touched us too closely, hadn't wanted to stay and watch, but we were trapped by the crowd of spectators who stood with breathless grief to see the two policemen striding so ominously along the middle of the road with the red striped canvas bundle slung between them. The air seemed to grow colder as the policemen approached, passed by and turned into the gate of Granny Jones's house where Bobbie had lived and only after the door of the house had closed behind the sad cortège did the crowd break up into small, weeping, head-shaking murmuring groups.

'It was meant to be,' said a woman behind us.

'It's funny, right enough,' said another.

Fran and I ran from the scene and not until we met Cora by the low railings outside Parr's Bank did we stop for breath. Cora's eyes were wide and bright.

'It's funny it should be him, isn't it?' she said, and when we couldn't understand she gave us her version of the story.

Bobbie's mother had been a bad woman. How bad, Cora didn't really know, but bad enough to attempt, when Bobbie was only three months old, to drown him by throwing him into a bath of cold water. Only his father's opportune arrival had saved Bobbie and he had immediately been taken away to be brought up by his granny. Although he must have been too young for the incident to have affected him the strange thing was that the boy had grown up with an unreasoning fear of water. Even the Saturday tub in front of the fire had seemed to terrify him and he had been over five years old before he could be persuaded to sit in the water. When, therefore, Bobbie had come and asked his granny if he might go with some of his schoolmates to the third landing she hadn't hesitated, knowing that with his fear of water he wasn't likely to come to any harm.

'He didn't even paddle while we were there,' interrupted Fran. 'He stayed on the bank. I know because I heard the boys calling him "cowardy custard".' Cora nodded the interruption away, telling us that his schoolmates had confirmed that Bobbie didn't go into the water and that he'd come all the way back home with them before he found he'd lost his penknife and said he was going back to look for it. The boys had told him not to go back then, that they would accompany him the following afternoon and help him search. He had seemed satisfied with their promise but he must have changed his mind later and trudged back those lonely three miles to the third landing where his body was found.

'And what's stranger,' Cora went on, 'is that though he was terrified of water they found all his clothes on the bank and the penknife in his pocket That's why they're saying it was meant to be.'

I suppose Fran and I still looked puzzled because she explained. 'They say the water called him.'

I shivered. 'I don't want to go to the third landing again,' I said.

'Nor me,' said Fran.

Shortly after Bobbie's death the authorities erected barbed-wire fences and hired a watchman to see that no intruders ventured on the forbidden territory and picnickings, paddlings and wave-jumpings at the third landing ceased altogether. You couldn't even go and sit on the banks and get a vestige of sun-tan.

9

Telephones were scarce in the town and public call-boxes completely lacking. If you needed to telephone, and need was the operative word, you had to go to the General Post Office, which, though it had been regarded as centrally situated when it was first built, had become steadily more isolated as the main business and residential areas of the town spread away from the stagnating docks and reached 'above the railway station'. The post office telephone was accessible to the public only during opening hours and if outside those hours there was an urgent need to telephone you had to knock at the door of the postmaster's private flat above and have him relay the message. As the postmaster was deaf, understandably testy and irrepressibly curious, people preferred to go to the police station which was cosier and ask there for a message to be sent through; at least the policemen weren't deaf.

Father frequently considered the idea of having a telephone installed at the shop. It would undoubtedly have been a boon when we were running short of some commodity or other to lift the phone and instruct the wholesaler to send out a consignment on the next train, but in view of the cost of its installation and the subsequent rental he was unable to convince himself that the telephone was vitally necessary. Not, that is, until the exciting day we landed the hospital contract. Every year the local paper carried an advertisement inserted by the hospital authorities inviting tenders for the supply of provisions, always, of course, with the proviso that 'The committee did not bind itself to accept the lowest or any tender'. Father had not bothered to submit a tender because it was generally believed that the invitation was a mere formality, the contract invariably being placed with a well-established grocer who was a close relative of the matron. He was pleasantly mystified, therefore, when a member of the committee during what appeared to be a casual visit to the shop expressed surprise that Father had not made any attempt to secure such a coveted order. With a heavy wink the committee member had advised him to do so next time the advertisement appeared. Somewhat sceptically Father accepted the advice and set to work calculating the most attractive terms he could offer before posting off his tender. Three weeks went by during which time my parents waited with carefully suppressed optimism until a letter marked

'Hospital Tenders' arrived. Mother and I watched the look of delight that spread over Father's face as he digested the news that the hospital contract was his for the ensuing twelve months. For him it was the accolade. A shop had to have built up a considerable reputation to have been chosen as the first supplier to have wrested the order from the matron's relative and he had achieved it after a relatively short time. He was as jubilant as if he had been granted a 'By Royal Appointment' and promised Mother she could buy a new sitting-room suite on the strength of it.

It now became imperative for us to have a telephone, since it was the matron's custom to phone the hospital order through daily and without further debate, Father got in touch with the post office. Within a day or two there the instrument stood in a little cubby-hole that had been cleared for it among the shelves at the back of the shop and less than a quarter of an hour after its installation Father was briskly turning the handle that rang the exchange and asking for the number of his wholesaler in Liverpool. Mother, with a lenient smile, accused him of having purposely let the sugar supply run low so that he would have an excuse to use the telephone but this Father indignantly denied.

We were soon to discover that having the only telephone in the neighbourhood brought its disadvantages. Customers and non-customers alike no longer thought it necessary to walk all the way to the post office to telephone but nipped in to use ours, disturbing us at mealtimes, in the evenings when the shop was closed and knocking us up at night when it was an urgent call for the doctor. 'Isn't it handy!' they exclaimed, and obviously so much regarding the instrument as a communal one that some people appeared affronted when Father reminded them that he, and therefore they, had to pay for the privilege. At first Father charged the same amount for a call as was shown on his telephone bill, but the increasing number of callers became such a nuisance

he resolved to charge non-customers the same as they would
have to pay for the public telephone at the post office. This
cut down the number of applicants and thereafter our private
life became more tolerable. However the number of incom-
ing calls, asking that messages, both serious and trifling,
should be conveyed to residents in the locality, did not
diminish and until he was disillusioned Father judged it
good policy to oblige whenever possible. If I was at home, it
was often my job, as I was the person most easily spared, to
convey these messages and since I was sometimes given a
sweet or a bunch of flowers or even a penny by the recipient
as a reward for my trouble, and since I was enabled to peep
into homes where otherwise I might never have a chance to
visit, I was perfectly happy with the arrangement.

It was through a telephone message that I came into
contact with the Bensons, who had formed themselves into a
pierrot troupe in which every member of the family took an
active part. Father Benson did the stage-managing; Mother
Benson played the piano and made the costumes; the four
daughters acted and danced and sang; the elder son wrote
simple sketches, taking any comic parts himself, and the
younger son played the violin. Their home was always
overflowing with music and laughter so that as soon as I got
within fifty yards of the front door I could feel my feet
tingling and my body shaping itself to dance. Except for the
youngest sister and brother who were still at school the
Bensons all worked at shops or factories and so pushed were
they to find time for rehearsals they used to go through their
patter while eating a meal, as I found one evening when I
had to go there at teatime. The message I took concerned a
show they were putting on that evening and it needed a reply
which I was to take back. Invited to wait inside while Father
and Mother Benson discussed the message to be sent I was
able to watch and listen to the rest of the family, already
dressed in their pierrot costumes, happily rehearsing their

lines, chaffing and applauding each other as they cut up slices of brawn on their plates, dug forks into a jar of pickles, gulped thick slices of bread and butter and sucked up mouthfuls of tea. They were a sparklingly happy family on stage and off and while admitting they had little of the glamour of a show at the Hippodrome I became one of their most devoted admirers. It cost only a penny to go and see the Benson pierrots and as often as pocket money permitted I contrived to be there, sitting in the front row and clapping as often as I knew applause was expected. I had learned by heart virtually every line of every speech and song; I mimicked their gestures and practised their dances whenever I could find a place safe from the surveillance of my parents; familiarity bred not contempt but enthusiasm and I enjoyed the show all the more for knowing in advance what was to come.

Eventually the Bensons sensed that their appeal in the town was waning and rather than give up the hobby they loved and enjoyed so much they gave up their jobs and their home and bought an old wagon which they fitted out as both living quarters and substitute stage. Complete with props and piano and buoyant with aspiration the family set out *en masse* to tour remote towns and villages up and down the country where, they were confident, there would still be a welcome for their brand of entertainment.

Into the Bensons' former home moved a family of boorish sour-voiced 'Up Wummers' and the only sounds that emanated from the once exuberant house were those of a scrubbing brush on the floors or a donkey stone on the steps. Father assessed them and promptly dubbed them as 'Co op types' because of their churlishness and suspiciousness which seemed to be afflictions most prevalent among people who dealt exclusively with the Co-operative Society's shops. I certainly did not expect to be visiting the old Benson home again, but after the 'Up Wummers' had been in residence little more than a month Father announced when I came home from school one day that there was a telephone message for the son of the house. It was apparently a message from his lady friend telling him she would be off duty at a certain time and instructing him to meet her at a specified place. I skipped off to the 'Up Wummers' house, delivered the message, had the door slammed in my face the moment I had finished speaking, and returned home. Two days later there was another similar message which I also delivered. The following week there were two more and thus it continued. As neither the young lady's family nor the 'Up Wummers' ever showed their faces inside our shop Father felt they had a fearful cheek in expecting to be danced attendance on and he grumbled every time he replaced the receiver after the girl had telephoned. Notwithstanding, someone was always despatched with the message, usually me, and never once did I get a sweet or even a smile or a 'thank you' for my pains. Indeed on one occasion when I was unsure about the exact time the young lady wished to be met the son of the house sneered and accused me of a lack of brains, which stung me into replying that he didn't deserve to have messages brought to him. The next time I heard his young lady's voice on the telephone I was about to dash off to get myself a new hair ribbon in readiness for the school concert the next day but I thought I might just as well take the message first. To my consternation I heard Father saying petulantly that he would not take any more such calls; that he was far too busy running a business to run a 'spooning market' and that in any case he had no one available to send. I almost found myself protesting since despite my frosty receptions at the house I had secretly enjoyed playing the role of cupid in a love affair and now that it was to cease I felt a sense of deposal. Much later I learned the reason for Father's veto. Word had reached him that the young man had got the girl into trouble and Father thought that, through the telephone, we were somehow implicated. Subsequently he refused to accept such frivolous messages for anyone, so I never got the chance to play cupid again but was only sent to convey information about proposed visits of relatives or births or illness and on one memorable occasion a death.

When Father was requested to acquaint old Mrs Wright with the fact that her husband had died suddenly he was dubious about sending me. He thought I was too young to be the bearer of such momentous news and asked Mother if she would go. Mother flatly refused, saying that Mrs Wright would 'keep her canting till dinner-time'. Canting' was just talking or gossiping and was what, according to Mother, many of our neighbours did most of the day long. Wearing a clean apron to signify that household chores were finished, they liked to stand on their front doorsteps for hours on end, scrutinising and commenting on all the activities of the street. Since the errand boys were out on long deliveries there was no alternative but to send me, so Father, thinking it might save both Mrs Wright and me embarrassment, wrote the tidings on a sheet of paper, folded it carefully and instructed me to hand it in and come away immediately. I sped off, conscious of a little thrill at being the bearer of eventful news, but as I neared Mrs Wright's house I remembered to walk more sedately and to compose my features in the degree of glumness I thought the situation required. I lifted the brass knocker three distinct times, thinking it sounded fateful, and when the door opened I silently handed the old lady the note and turned to go away. She called my name.

'Wait a minute, dearie. Just let's see if there's an answer.'

I maintained my glum expression and watched her as she read. For a moment she appeared incredulous but then she turned and called loudly up the stairs.

'Maisie! Come down here! The old bugger's dead at last!'

I was horrified. Swearing at any time was wicked but swearing over a dead husband sounded diabolical. I turned hastily away but Mrs Wright caught my sleeve insistently. Her other hand was delving into the pocket of her apron from which she produced a leather purse. I felt acutely uncomfortable. I didn't want a reward for taking news of a death but the old lady was already holding out her hand on the palm of which lay a silver half-crown. I drew back.

'Oh, yes, you must, dearie. You've brought me the best bit of news I've had in twenty years.'

I stared at the half-crown. It was an enormous amount. Mrs Wright took my speechlessness for reluctance and pushed the coin into the pocket of my coat. She smiled benignly at me and closed the door. I forgot to be glum and raced back home where my parents stared at each other with a dismay that, with Father at any rate, I could see concealed amusement.

'She ought not to have said such a thing in front of a young girl!' exclaimed Mother indignantly. I wondered what she would have said if I had repeated the actual profanity Mrs Wright had used but I had not dared. To have been too literal might have jeopardised my half-crown.

'I expect she had a drop too much to drink last night,' Father said in extenuation. He turned to me. 'You mustn't ever tell anyone else about this,' he cautioned, explaining at the same time that Mrs Wright's husband had been a reprobate old drunkard and had deserted her years ago. Now he was dead she'd most likely be better off because she'd get a regular pension.

A week later I was astonished to see in our local newspaper under the 'Deaths' column, of which I was an avid reader, the name of 'John Wright—dearly beloved husband of Emma Wright'. A year later, on the anniversary of his death, I was equally astonished to see under the 'In Memoriam' column a loving tribute to the deceased John Wright, incorporating a tender verse and ending with the words 'Sadly missed by his loving wife and daughter Maisie', and on each succeeding anniversary, until Mrs Wright herself died, a simil: notice was inserted.

Such hypocrisy perplexed me so much I eventually confided my secret to Fran. I was back at my old school now so that Fran and I had been able to resume our steady companionship. It was a Saturday afternoon and we were sitting astride a low branch of elm which overhung a weedy pond, our habitual refuge in hot and sticky weather and a place that was conducive to the atmosphere of a confessional. Fran sucked in a shocked breath when I had finished.

'Maybe she's awful sorry now that he's really dead,' she suggested. 'Maybe she's suffering agonies of penance like the mother in *East Lynn*.' We had clandestinely been reading *East Lynn* and improbable as it may sound we let our imaginations slip fat, boozy old Mrs Wright into the beautiful, tragic character whose ultimate fate had made us weep on each other's shoulders. 'I expect Mr Wright reads those notices in heaven and he'll know she's very sorry,' said Fran.

I wondered if drunkards such as Mr Wright was reputed to have been ever got to heaven, but Fran, being the daughter of a publican, was emphatic that they did.

She reached up for a higher branch and swung herself up on to it. I was too cowardly to follow suit and the branch I was on was as far as I dared risk. Fran stared down at me through the leaves.

'Did you say she gave you a whole half-crown?' she demanded in an awestruck voice.

'Yes. I didn't want to take it but she put it in my pocket.'

Fran adjusted her position on the branch. 'Have you spent it?' she asked.

'No, it's still in my money-box.' I was saving up for a gold tooth or a bicycle; I wasn't sure which.

Fran's next remark shook me so much I nearly toppled from my perch.

'I think you should get it out and use it for buying flowers to put on Mr Wright's grave,' she advised. 'Half a crown will buy lots of nice flowers for lots of weeks and everybody will think it's Mrs Wright doing it.'

I suffered a moment of anguish before memory came up with a retort that meant a blessed reprieve for my half-crown. 'I can't do that,' I said, shaking my head.

'Why not?' asked Fran.

I stemmed the exultation in my voice. 'Because he's buried in Birmingham,' I told her.

My interest in the 'In Memoriam' column did not cease with the discovery of Mrs Wright's apparent duplicity, but though the tears still came to my eyes when I came across a particularly affecting sentiment I grew to regard any notice that mourned a spouse over forty years old with a certain amount of irreverence. It was with such feelings I perceived one week the name of 'Nellie Bain'.

In a long row of terraced houses not far from the shop there had lived a middle-aged Mr and Mrs Bain. Right next door to them had come to live a middle-aged but well-dressed and attractive widow whose name was Mrs Copley. Mrs Bain was an invalid and local gossip soon had it that Mr Bain was finding solace in the company of Mrs Copley. Indeed several people suspected that a portion of the high brick wall that separated the adjoining backyards of their houses had not, as Mr Bain maintained, suddenly fallen down of its own accord but that Mr Bain had systematically weakened the foundations so as to cause its collapse and thus make a convenient gap which enabled him to visit the widow without exposing himself to the censuring eyes of neighbours. Within a year or two of Mrs Copley's appearance Mrs Bain died and after a prudent period of mourning the widow became the new Mrs Bain. For about eighteen months the couple appeared happy enough together and then people began to comment on Mr Bain's harassed expression and the fact that he was growing noticeably thinner. Rumour soon had it that he had discovered his new wife to be a mean and carping woman. As she was a customer of ours we had been aware of her true nature for some time and indeed it seemed that Mr Bain himself was the only person to have been in ignorance of the sharp-voiced stinginess and the preoccupation with stylish clothes which had made her unpopular with the neighbours almost from the first week of her arrival. Speculation on the state of affairs between the two became a slyly amusing topic of conversation among the customers who thronged the shop on Friday and Saturday evenings, particularly when the wife of one of Mr Bain's workmates reported that Mr Bain was constantly complaining he was starved of a good meal and that his wife secretly rifled his pockets so that he could never find a copper to go for a drink with his mates. His most bitter complaint, however, was that she had cancelled the pigeon peas and thirds which in his first wife's time had been regular items on their weekly grocery order, telling him he could buy the pigeon food out of his drink money or else get rid of the pigeons which she detested and Mr Bain loved. As the strife between the couple became more and more marked the gossip about them increased.

Our local paper was published on Friday evenings and the shop was at its busiest when I darted in, waving the paper and trying to call Father's attention to the 'In Memoriam' column. I was not supposed to go into the shop for frivolous reasons when they were busy, and Father, who was listening sceptically to some customer who was whining about being short of money, was about to admonish me for interrupting when his eye fell on the name I was pointing to so eagerly.

'Nellie Bain!' I whispered fiercely. Now Mr Bain's wife had been dead for three years without so much as a word of lamentation being published by her husband but here he was proclaiming her to be the 'sorely missed wife of the ever devoted Edward Bain'. Mother took the paper from me and ironically read out the notice. Father banished me with a nod but not before I had time to hear expostulations of 'Well, I never!' and 'That's a bob in the eye all right!' which were always the standard comments on any interesting or puzzling situation.

No one was much surprised when, a few months later on what was estimated to be the tenth anniversary of his death, the former and hitherto mute Mrs Copley retaliated by inserting a notice in memory of her first husband, describing herself as 'his ever sorrowing widow, Bessie'. The following year Nellie Bain's memoriam notice declared she had been 'the best wife a man ever had'. People were agog to know what the late Mr Copley had been and they were not disappointed. When the second 'In Memoriam' notice appeared it transpired he had been 'a gem on God's earth, now lost forever'. Father, who had been acquainted with Mr Copley, commented that 'gem' was probably a misprint for 'germ' which he thought would have been a more fitting description. Much to the interest and amusement of neighbours the rival 'In Memoriam' notices, with sentiments growing ever more eulogistic as the discord between the couple increased, continued for five years, when Mr Bain withdrew from the conflict by making his wife a widow for the second time. Thereafter the widow was content to mourn either or both her husbands with more privacy and less expense.

'I wonder how she feels now she's lost two good husbands?' observed Mother as she watched the black-clad widow passing the house on her way to church one Sunday.

Father let slip a wry grin. 'I'm wondering how the editor of the paper feels now he's lost two good customers.'

The saddest message I had to take was to Horatio's home. 'Horatio' was the nickname of the rag-and-bone man and it was Father who for some obscure reason had dubbed him thus. He was a tall, bony man with a sucked-in face, a soggy moustache that caught his perpetual dewdrop, and spectacles with lenses as thick as the jam jars people took to his cart. We never seemed to have any rags or bones to dispose of but I was occasionally allowed to escort other children when they took jam jars, old sacks, old shoes and bones to Horatio's cart to be exchanged for a copper or two. He was a silent unsmiling man and for a long time I thought he was dumb as well as half blind since I never heard him speak even to give a command to the wiry little pony who pulled the large cart as easily as if it were a baby's perambulator. However, Father used to talk to Horatio and it was to Father he confided his ambition to give up rag and boning and become a farmer. In fact the opportunity had already come his way. He had put his savings into a half-share of a smallholding and within a month he and his wife were to move in. The pony for which he had a great affection was to be retired and live out his life in one of the fields.

So Horatio and his pony and cart disappeared from the streets for about two years until it was discovered that the smallholding had been heavily in debt when Horatio had taken his partnership and that his savings had merely helped to temporarily stave off bankruptcy. Out came the pony and cart from retirement and once again Horatio was back on the streets, rag and boning again to pay off his debts, even more blind and less communicative than before, though his dewdrop had not deserted him.

It was in the dusk of a winter's evening that the message came through that Horatio had been killed. It appeared he had been racing his cart homeward over some crossroads when a lorry came out and crashed into him. Both Horatio and his pony were killed outright. I was older now and deemed capable of relaying such messages, so I was sent to the smallholding with the news. Cora joined me on the way and I was grateful for her company. When I knocked at the door it was answered by a white-haired, spotlessly clean woman whose eyes were tight shut and it came as a shock to both Cora and me to realise that Mrs Horatio was blind. It made my task seem even more depressing and difficult. Just as I was about to speak, however, a young man on a bicycle came racing up the path.

'What d'you want?' he demanded of us, somewhat truculently.

'There's a message,' I began timidly.

'I know,' he snapped. 'Thank you all the same.'

Thankfully I saw him lead the old woman back into the house and close the door.

10

All the year round there were events, scheduled or un-
scheduled, to which the children of the town flocked like
gulls to a fish pier; unique occasions like the felling of the
sky-high brickworks chimney which Father insisted I get up
early to witness because he suspected I might never have such
an opportunity again; the transporting of an enormous tree-
trunk to the local timber yard for which fifteen heavy shire

horses had to be specially hired; exhilarating occasions like the summer fêtes and carnivals; the weekly parade of the brass band, and intermittent processions of the more colourful though infinitely less tuneful jazz bands. There were everyday sights too, which, though relatively unimpressive, were still compelling enough to make us abandon play and rush to witness them: the water cart which in summer sprayed the dusty streets and sometimes our legs when we ventured deliberately close; the rag-and-bone man who gave windmills in exchange for jam jars and old clothes; the cockleman who, when there was an 'R' in the month, spent his time selling shellfish from an open cart. When there was no 'R' in the month he spent his time in prison for ill-treating either his wife or his horse. There were the Saturday-night street services of the Salvation Army when the band played spirited hymn tunes and we literally danced attendance, and there was the spectacle of the ragged-trousered paper boys, hopping from one bare foot to the other as they impatiently awaited the arrival of the train with the evening newspapers.

Fran and I liked to go down to the station in time to hear the first ringing of the bell in the signal-box which warned of the oncoming train and to watch the signalman turning the heavy wheel that closed the level crossing to traffic. As soon as we heard the crash of the big levers we would look along the line to see the signal arms dip like a salute. As the train steamed in we waved to the engine driver and fireman while we peered to catch a glimpse of the savage flames in the engine fire-box. Before the train had brayed to a full stop the paper boys flew at the parcels of disgorged papers like starving hens at a single grain of corn, bickering, squealing and fighting so that the newsagent in charge had to virtually throw his body over the papers to protect them. As he divided them into bundles the boys snatched them from him and with incredible speed raced off, yelling incomprehensively, bare feet scudding along the platform, over the rails and into the streets.

In winter, when we were discouraged from going near the station, Fran and I sometimes liked to follow the lamplighter on part of his round, watching him set up his ladder, climb up to the lamp, clean it, lift the hinged glass and put a match to the mantle. The lamplighter was Welsh and used to sing most appropriately 'All things bright and beautiful' while he worked and seemed pleased enough when we joined in. Later we might attach ourselves to a band of children to play the special winter evening games for which darkness was essential: 'Dicky-Dicky-shine-a-light' when one group of children with a lighted candle in a perforated cocoa tin were hunted by another group, or we might indulge in a mild form of 'Dare and Do' which was usually nothing more heinous than knocking on someone's door and running away before it was opened or going into a draper's shop to ask for samples of baby ribbon.

One winter Fran and I discovered the 'Gospel Tent' to which we could only gain admittance by squirming under the big marquee after the service had started and the attention of the congregation was concentrated on the hungry-looking minister who preached frenziedly, prayed tearfully and played passionately on his 'cello for the hymn-singing. It was really the 'cello that intrigued us and the way the minister played it as if he were trying to cut tough meat with a blunt knife. The minister, who ate and slept in the tent, became a customer at the shop and complaining that his 'cello got damp he asked if he might store it in our spare room. When at the end of his mission he finally came to collect it and to say goodbye he brought me a present of a white, lacy pinafore which I dubbed my 'Gospel Tent pinny'. My parents thought I looked so angelic in it that Father stood me on a chair and took a photograph of me.

Most of the churches and chapels ran 'socials' once or twice a month for the benefit of children attending their Sunday schools, but Fran and I discovered that the organisers were non-sectarian when it came to accepting admission fees, so with complete impartiality we attended Methodist, Roman Catholic, Salvation Army and Church of England socials and I can recall only one occasion when we did not particularly enjoy ourselves. It was a Wesleyan social and was blighted from the start by the determination of the minister to appoint himself master of ceremonies, but the trouble did not begin until we were chosen to join a team of five children under the supervision of a Sunday school teacher to play a kind of charades. In this case the word chosen was 'table' and each of us was given a letter of the word and told to choose a street, market or fairground cry to illustrate it. Fran went first and stood in front of the drawn curtains of the stage. She chanted in a sing-song voice:

> 'Twopence a time. Twopence a time.
> Come on, boys, twopence a time.'

No doubt the minister and his cronies believed her to be imitating a barker at a coconut shy, but we knew that 'Twopence a time' was the nickname of a much painted and powdered lady with fiercely hennaed hair who was in the habit of patrolling the vicinities of factories and pubs on pay night and Fran was imitating the cheeky chant set up by children who observed her. We were not, of course, aware of any significance in the nickname. To us she was 'Twopence' or 'Twopence a time' and we accepted it as unquestioningly as we accepted nicknames like 'Totty Russell' and 'Reasty Dick' and 'Jinny Lightning'.

When my turn came I had the letter 'B' and wanting to do at least as well as Fran I barged through the curtains shouting: 'Billy's Weekly Liar; twopence. Come on, lads, bust your buttons; ladies, bust your bodices. Life's all fun with Billy's Weekly Liar.' Before I could finish two hands gripped my shoulders and hauled me back through the curtains where I was confronted with a flushed Sunday school teacher who said she was ashamed of me and asked what the minister would think. I, believing there could be nothing wrong in imitating a cry which the minister could have heard every Friday outside the market, immediately went into a sulk when Fran comforted me by saying she thought I'd been jolly good but that the Sunday school teacher was hoping the minister would marry her and she was afraid of upsetting him.

The next upset occurred at refreshment time when the minister told us to bow our heads while he said grace and my mouth was already crammed full of cake. It was a long grace and the cake was flavoured with almonds which I hated. I wanted to spit it out into my paper napkin but fearing it would rustle I had to wait until the minister had finished and by that time the taste of almonds in my mouth had put me off the rest of the food. Before the end of the social I was at the stage of detesting that minister with his floppy voice and weakly gesticulating hands directing us what to do and spoiling our fun and it was the last straw when he asked us to kneel while he prayed God to make us good and watch over us on the way home. Fran and I had planned not to be good on the way home and we had collected pocketfuls of paper cake cups which we intended pushing through letter boxes before we knocked and ran away. But fearing God might answer the latter part of the minister's prayer and be watching us we stuffed the cake cups instead into an empty collection box that stood on a table in the porch.

Sometimes the socials were distinguished by the name of 'Flower Socials' when each child was given a small posy of flowers to take home. Others were called 'Supper Socials' which indicated that the food was to be a little more substantial than that at an ordinary social, and then there were 'Cobweb Socials', which Fran and I found least resistible. For these events the 'Cobweb' woven of stout string covered the entire ceiling of the hall and as children were admitted they were each given a dangling strand which they had to pull gently, coiling it round and round their hands as it unwove from the cobweb and led them hither and thither about the hall until, coming to the end of their string, they would find a welcome pack of sweets attached to it. Occasionally when a child was over-exuberant there might be a tangle but mostly they were so absorbed in watching the steady unweaving of the cobweb it was the adults in charge who grew impatient and urged that the string should be pulled more strongly.

Socials were interspersed with 'Potato Pie Suppers' or concerts given by local amateurs, but these were rare treats for me because it was almost my bedtime before they started. Fran, whose bedtime was later than mine, used to teach me any good songs she'd heard at the concerts so that we could sing them together and made me hungry describing the 'Potato Pie Suppers'.

Friday nights were market nights and Fran and I went regularly to see the flare-lit stalls spread with merchandise and attended by bawling stallkeepers. We joined the crowd watching the crockery merchant banging his crockery on a tea-chest as he gradually whittled down the price he had asked initially for the goods; we listened to the patent-medicine man who, in all weathers, stood with bare torso showing off his muscled brown body which he claimed he had achieved by regular doses of the medicine he was selling. Like most of the onlookers we knew his spiel off by heart; knew the moment his accomplice would be invited to punch him hard in the solar plexus to demonstrate how tough was his body. It looked a lovely punch; the crowd gasped at the 'sonk!' as it landed and debilitated youths and feeble old men among his listeners grew restive in their eagerness to proffer a shilling in exchange for one of the small black bottles.

There were many characters at the market, such as the gypsy whose 'stall' was a couple of portmanteaus in which he kept his stock of herbal remedies. He too was a splendid figure of a man with black curly hair clustered round his head-dress and bristling up from the open neck of his shirt, which I at first had thought was a black cat. Women loved the gypsy, though Fran and I thought he was very rude. If a woman asked for corn cure he would openly deride her for wearing silly shoes and tell her only God could cure such stupidity; when someone asked for watercress ointment which he hadn't brought that evening he told her, 'Why do you buy that stuff from me when you can buy lard from the shop and pick watercress from the brook?'

'What do I do then?' bleated the woman.

'Use your common sense, if you've got any. Boil 'em up together for half an hour, strain it and let it set. Anything else you want to know?'

The woman smirked and thanked him effusively. The crowd murmured their appreciation and closed in around him ready to buy whatever potions or ointment he had to sell.

The haberdashery stall was kept by a narrow-eyed, narrow-nosed old man who every week selected two young boys from among the urchins who loitered around the market place to stand at the front of his stall holding a tray of oddments and shouting, 'All on this tray—one penny'. Normally there was great competition for this honour particularly since the old man was reputed to pay each boy sixpence. However, one night when Fran and I were at the market rather earlier than usual, we noticed there were no young barkers to be seen. It was Fran's idea that we should offer our services. The old man eyed us distastefully for a moment but handed us each a tray and told us to begin shouting. After the first few minutes I grew uneasy. Customers from the shop were among the crowds and they were staring at me in my new role. One actually stopped and demanded to know what my father would say if he could see me. I knew very well what my father would say and since I could see Fran too was beginning to have second thoughts about the wisdom of our idea we both put down our trays and told the old man we didn't want to work for him any more. Nevertheless we waited hopefully. We knew we hadn't earned sixpence each but we thought he might perhaps give us threepence between us. Instead he muttered uncomplimentary remarks about girls under his breath and presented me with a knot of tape and Fran with a packet of pins which, under the circumstances, we knew we dared not risk taking home. I suggested we should give them to the woebegone little man outside the market place who regularly pumped out hymn tunes on a chesty concertina and had a notice like an apron tied round his waist, which read, 'Invalid wife and four children to support.' Fran thought it a good idea because the man was such a good customer at their pub but that made me oppose it. She suggested we ask the 'Billy's Weekly Liar' man to give us a 'Liar' in exchange but as I knew I dared not take home a 'Liar' either we startled the old soldier playing a musical saw by tossing them into the cap that lay inviting pennies on the pavement beside him.

Fortunately for me my escapade at the market never reached the ears of my parents.

Nor I am glad to say did they ever hear of my perfidy at the time of the General Election. Our town was overwhelmingly Tory. My parents were staunch Tory; my grandmother's parlour was the Tory committee room; the butcher, the baker and the dustbinman wore Tory rosettes and even our washerwoman who slaved at the washtub until she herself looked as if she had been boiled and bleached in a strong solution of soda was unswerving in her loyalty to the Tory candidate. The main opposition came from the Liberal Party, Labour then being only a feeble voice in the wilderness. A stranger passing through the town could have easily discerned its political leanings by the fact that the posters depicting the Liberal and Labour candidates were invariably mud-spattered or defaced while those showing the Tory candidate remained unsullied. The colours representative of the parties were yellow for Labour, blue for Liberal and, surprisingly, red for Conservative, and though my parents conscientiously avoided any open manifestation of their political views in case customers were offended, at election time I was allowed to wear red ribbon bows in my hair and a conspicious red rosette pinned to my dress which display could be dismissed as a childish whim. To anyone commenting on it Father replied, 'Oh, she just likes the colour.' It was true. I did like the colour, particularly since Fran wore a contrasting large blue rosette as her parents voted Liberal. Cora's parents were listless Labour and Cora when she was allowed to be our companion would have liked to complete the tricolour by sporting a Labour rosette but as her mother wouldn't give her the money to buy ribbon and neither Fran nor I after searching our family ragbags could produce anything suitable Cora had to be content with wearing the nearest thing to a yellow rosette she could find which was the palm cross given to her by the Sunday school.

The evening before the Election I was sent to Grandmother's house with a message from my parents and to my astonishment found several people clustered around her garden gate. Granny flushed and fluttering with excitement and wearing her best black skirt and blouse, met me in the lobby with the news that she was expecting at any moment a visit from the Tory candidate. I had barely seated myself on the kitchen stool when from the street came an animated babble of voices interspersed with hearty cheering and the noise of a car engine. Granny went to the front door and peeping out from the kitchen I saw the handsome Tory candidate alighting from the car and handing out his beautiful young wife. I was darting upstairs, hoping to get a better view from the landing, when to my consternation I was spotted and called down to be presented. While the candidate and his wife exclaimed enthusiastically over my eye-catching bows and rosette I stood shy and speechless and had difficulty in unsticking my dry tongue to answer their questions as to my name, how old I was and if I was always such a good little Tory. I trailed behind the party as Granny's parlour was approved, the mantelpiece crammed with glass pigs which Great-Grandfather had had a penchant for blowing was admired and Granny herself complimented on the arrangements she had made for the comfort of the Election committee. I inserted myself between a high backed chair and the window, hoping the neighbours would be able to see how closely I was concerned with the proceedings, and as I stared at the handsome black car with its polished brass headlamps and the uniformed chauffeur waiting beside it the extravagant, intoxicating hope was born that since Granny was doing so much to help the Tory party and since I so flagrantly displayed its colours, the candidate and his wife might possibly invite me to ride home with them. I visualised myself seated between them, nodding and waving regally to bystanders as the car proceeded slowly along the main street. I imagined the look of amazement on Father's face when I was deposited outside the shop.

'Come along, it's time for you to go home.' Granny's voice cut into my dreams and because Granny was old and gentle and kind I neither wheedled nor argued but went quietly on my way. But I walked slowly, still cherishing the hope that, in full view of all the onlookers, the big car would draw up beside me and I should be invited to ride home. Hope faded as I neared home and when my attention was caught by a mustering of children outside 'Daddy Handcart's' I forgot my daydream and full of curiosity crossed the road to investigate. 'Daddy Handcart's' was a second-hand shop, packed with fossilised clamjamphrie that was scarcely visible through the grime that covered the windows like a blind. The space left for a customer to stand was minute and trade was negligible because if someone wanted an item from the heterogeneity of stock fat old Mrs 'Handcart' after recovering from the palpitating shock of being confronted by a customer would hold up her hands in a gesture of helplessness and in a whimpering foreign voice attempt to inveigle them into first buying everything that was piled on top of the desired object for fear the whole agglomeration should collapse. The inveiglement was so insistent on occasion it was tantamount to a refusal to sell, as a disgruntled would-be customer explained to Father. 'When you go in to ask for a coal scuttle you don't expect to have to buy a commode, a three-legged chair, a fiddle with one string and a couple of spittoons as well but the woman doesn't seem able to take no for an answer.'

Father grinned. 'What did she expect you to do?' he asked. 'Keep coal in the commode and sit on the three-legged chair playing the one string fiddle while you filled up both spittoons?' The customer was over-refined and looked shocked.

'You shouldn't have said that about the spittoons,' Mother reproved Father afterwards. 'She didn't think it was very funny.'

'She wouldn't,' said Father. 'She comes from Wolverhampton.'

'Daddy Handcart' was himself an eccentric-looking character with long greasy black hair sometimes tucked into a bun beneath a shabby cap; a dusty black beard that always looked as if it had been freshly treated with Keatings Powder and combative black eyes. He was either too proud or too militant to be employed, regarding himself as belonging to the 'boss' rather than the working class and though he must have contrived to earn a living somehow during the day his only occupation seemed to be the restless pushing around of an empty handcart. In the evenings he was the town's most fervent Liberal, literally carrying his soap-box with him and mounting it to harangue fortuitous gatherings of people whether they were waiting for the level-crossing gates to open or merely gossiping at lamplit street corners.

As I approached the group of children Cora detached herself from them and came towards me. She was wearing an indisputable Liberal rosette and as I pointed an accusing finger she explained that 'Daddy Handcart' had given it to her because she was going to take part in a procession he was organising to march round the town carrying torches and chanting Liberal slogans. She started to recite:

'Put the Liberals in
And then you won't grow thin.
Put the Tories out
And watch yourself grow stout.'

She paused to see its effect on me. 'And he's giving us a bag of roasted chestnuts each when we've finished,' she added. 'Why don't you join in?'

I loved marching and chanting rhymes. I also loved roasted chestnuts which I never got at home because Father and Mother complained the bits got under their false teeth.

'Come on,' pressed Cora. 'It's only a bit of fun, after all.'

'I'll get into a row at home,' I demurred.

'They'll never know,' she assured me.

I knew I ought not to be tempted even for an instant but the procession promised to be such a dazzling one it was hard to resist. I made myself turn away but at that moment 'Daddy Handcart' and a couple of older children emerged from the back door of the shop carrying clusters of flaming torches which they distributed among the waiting children who received them with whoops and leaps of joy. It was too much for me. Furtively I removed the Tory rosette from my coat and stuffed it in a pocket. Taking up my position beside Cora I held out an eager hand for one of the resplendent torches.

'One, two, three, off we go!' called 'Daddy Handcart' and unfurling a large 'Vote Liberal' banner he took his place at the head of the procession. We moved off, stepping in time to our chanting and holding the torches high above our heads so that the evening breeze brushed their flaring flames. We had not gone far before we heard the sound of a motor engine and to my dismay a big black car, driven by a uniformed chauffeur, drew up beside us. I dodged behind Cora as the Tory candidate leaned out and addressed an affable quip in the direction of a glowering 'Daddy Handcart', but the girl immediately behind me started shrieking that I had nearly set her hair on fire with my torch and I was thumped back into my proper position. The shrieking had drawn the candidate's attention to me and it was with relief I saw his archly amused glance pass over me without a trace of recognition. He tapped a command to the chauffeur and as the car drew away I was sadly aware that the candidate's beautiful young wife was staring at me with a very puzzled expression on her face, as if she was trying to remember where she had seen me before.

II

Summer pastimes commenced towards the end of April
with the planning of the May Day processions which
entailed the choosing of the May Queen and her train-
bearers; the Maypole carrier and dancers, and, of course,
the collectors, the latter being children who could not
prevail upon their mothers to buy them light shoes for the
occasion. We made cardboard crowns for all the participants

with an extra special one for the May Queen; we made coloured paper flowers and stitched them to our dresses and to the long lace curtain, cajoled from someone's mother, which was the Queen's train. We decorated the Maypole—a broomstick—with paper streamers and a top-knot of flowers and our school playtimes and evenings were busy with rehearsals of our songs and dance steps. Back alleys resounded to our 'one-and-two-and-three-fours' and our 'Round and round the Maypole'; little May Queens looked coy as we crouched round them and sang:

> 'She's the Lily,
> The Lily Valley,
> She's the sweetest girl
> You've ever seen.
> She's the Lily,
> They call her (Norah),
> She's the Lily,
> The Lily Queen.'

Virtually every road and street where there were children had its May Queen procession and on the first of the month soon after midday dozens of small flower-bedecked bands of children set out in high spirits to trip and sing their way through the streets of the town, pausing every hour or so to fortify themselves with ice-cream pies bought with the money in the collecting boxes and returning at teatime limp and bedraggled, sometimes with the diminutive May Queen, wailing with tiredness, being given a 'fireman's lift' by two of the bigger girls.

On Saturday afternoon when the weather was too wet for play Fran and I were allowed to go to the matinées at the local Hippodrome. We were given fourpence each so that we could sit in the best seats at the front among the nice children but even so we had to get there early to be sure of being in the middle of a row. End seats were overhung by the 'penny balconies' which were the literal stamping ground of the rudest and scruffiest children of the neighbourhood whose favourite occupation during the show was spitting on the heads of the élite below. Once when Fran and I arrived too late for middle seats we went home with sticky, half-sucked toffees embedded in our hair and were banned from attending matinées for months.

Sometimes during the show the comedian announced a dancing or singing competition, inviting members of the audience to compete and offering a first prize of a shilling and a second prize of sixpence. There was invariably a rush of contestants from the 'penny balcony' for these events but no matter how talented they might be they rarely won a prize since it was the volume of applause that decided the winners and by withholding it we could extract vengeance for their maltreatment of us. On one occasion Fran, mainly because she was wearing a new bright pink dress which she wanted to be seen and admired, decided to compete. Apprehensively she followed the clamouring throng of galleryites through a curtained doorway and came out on to the stage. Fran's voice sounded like a wet finger being dragged on glass, but she looked so pretty, the audience, particularly the boys, applauded enthusiastically and she easily won first prize. The girl who won second prize was wearing a faded shawl, clogs, and black stockings spotted with holes; her little brother and sister, refusing to be left behind, were clinging to her shapeless dress as she moved to the front of the stage where she sang so beautifully that even I, whose normal reaction to singing was a fidgeting fit, knew that she should have won the contest. Even the actors and actresses on the stage seemed to be thrilled by the sound of her voice, but the children around me were whispering derisive comments on her appearance, and I, unable to overcome my disapproval of her appearing on a stage wearing clogs and holey stockings, refrained from showing approval of her singing.

Outside, after the show, Fran said: 'I thought that girl in the shawl would have won first prize but they seemed to like me better.' She skipped a few steps, making her skirt flop up and down. She turned to me. 'Did you like me best?' she demanded.

I shook my head miserably. 'You looked awfully nice but you couldn't sing like her.'

'But I was watching and you didn't clap for her; nor did anybody sitting near us.'

'That was because she wore clogs and had holes in her stockings,' I told her.

'Fancy going on a stage with holes in your stockings,' said Fran scornfully.

'Perhaps she's poor,' I said, 'and couldn't afford to buy darning wool.'

Fran looked suddenly horrified. 'D'you think she'd had any dinner?'

'Suppose she hasn't?' I murmured.

'Maybe that's why she sang so well. I've heard my dad telling people canaries sing best when they're hungry.'

'I hope she's not hungry,' I said. Our current reading was *My Neighbour's Shoes* and *The Water Babies* and with the intention of pleasing God via our favourite schoolmistress we were trying hard that week to emulate Aunt Martha and Mrs Doasyouwouldbedoneby.

'D'you think I'd be silly if I gave her sixpence out of my shilling?' asked Fran, and as it was her sacrifice rather than mine I responded with a glib headnodding. 'Come on,' she said and made towards the tiny shop inserted between the Hippodrome and a works canteen. She put her shilling on the counter and asked for two sixpences in exchange. 'We'll have to run to catch her up,' she said as we came out of the shop.

We found the girl coming out of a fruit shop and her brother and sister had already bitten deep into the apples she had given them.

Fran went up to her. 'I'd like you to have this sixpence,' she told the girl with all the aplomb of a practised do-gooder. 'My friend I and think you sang better than I did and you ought to have the shilling.'

The girl looked startled for a moment but she took the sixpence eagerly. Immediately her expression changed to one of hauteur. 'I should think a lot of people expected me to win it for your voice sounded to me no better than a horse fartin'.' She turned away dragging the two children with her.

'The cheek!' gasped Fran, blushing as bright a pink as her dress. Even before the blush had faded from her cheeks there was a glint of merriment in her eyes as she looked at me.

' "A horse fartin' ",' she repeated with a little gurgle of laughter in her voice.

'Farting's a dirty word,' I reproved.

'No, it's not, honestly,' she assured me. 'My dad says "fart" and "farting" so it must be all right.'

There were many things that Fran's father said that my parents certainly did not think were all right but I did not argue.

'Wait till my dad hears about this,' said Fran.

'About you winning the shilling?'

'No, about my voice being like a horse farting. He'll kill himself laughing.'

I wished I could tell my father.

It was an aunt of Fran's who kept the boarding house where the actors and actresses from the Hippodrome stayed and on Monday and Tuesday evenings when there were no performances we usually found some pretext for visiting the aunt and loitering near the over-scented parlour which was the artistes dining/sitting room. Rarely were the same actors and actresses there for more than three weeks at a time but they were invariably a kind and jolly crowd and on fine evenings they liked to sit outside on the steps or on the low garden wall chatting, singing, playing a concertina or a banjo and often several of them would get up and dance on the pavement. We admired them enormously. The women always wore lovely dresses and sparkling jewellery, their hair beautifully dressed. They made up, too, even to sit outside and though the chapel-going neighbours expressed mild disapproval and seemed to regard them as little more than vagabonds we liked nothing better than to crouch with our backs against the garden wall watching and listening, being taught to sing choruses and, if we showed any desire to join in their dancing, they painstakingly taught us the steps. They even invited Fran and me backstage at the Hippodrome, showing us the poky, grubby little rooms where they changed and made up and letting us find our way around all the exits and entrances. We were grateful for this introduction to backstage when the Hippodrome Christmas matinée came round and it was announced that the management were to give every child present a packet of chocolate and a halfpenny. As we left the theatre we had to pass a table in the entrance hall and here the manager and two usherettes handed out our gifts. Fran and I, knowing the secret of the backstage entrance, collected our halfpennies and chocolate, raced round to the stage door and through to the auditorium where we discreetly rejoined the outgoing flow of children. We kept up this performance until one of the usherettes screamed a challenge at us and we had to make a shamefaced retreat but by then we were each two-pence-halfpenny and five packets of chocolate the richer.

． ． ． ． ．

When the dark nights of winter came we went to the fair-ground. About a hundred yards to the rear of the shop there was an area of land which when we had first come to live in the vicinity had been totally enclosed and obscured by an intimidatingly high and rusty corrugated-iron fence. A year or two after our arrival the fence had been pulled down and we were able to see that the land from which we had been so strictly excluded was a pathetic waste of slablike soil, flecked here and there with determined clumps of stinkweed and hardly more attractive than the fence which had immured it. The new accessibility had two advantages, however: one that it provided a short cut for the workers on their way to and from the steelmills and the other that during all the years the council took to argue and vacillate over how best to utilise or dispose of the land it was available, during the winter months, to the amusement proprietors. Towards the end of October the throbbing, juddering steam engine arrived pulling a train of high-piled wagons and the caravans of the attendants, and within hours the waste ground was enclosed by hoopla stalls and booths of every description, the roundabouts were set up and the ground spread with sawdust. With the dusk the steam engine started to hiss and thump, the lights came on, dim at first but brightening as the engine gained confidence, and the fair was open.

It was the same people who came every year with the fair and since the proprietors, whose name was Clarkson, became customers at the shop for the duration of their stay and since Mrs Clarkson shared Mother's enthusiasm for whist drives they were considered by my parents to be respectable people and I was not debarred from fraternising. Indeed I was sometimes sent to deliver groceries to the Clarkson caravan and, once we had overcome our mutual suspicion, I was able to talk to the children and see at first hand how fairground people lived. I had always been brought up to regard people who lived in caravans as slatterns like the gypsies but the Clarkson caravan was a revelation. It was impeccably clean, with mirrors, woodwork and brass polished to a scintillating brilliance. The beds, screened by pretty curtains, were fresh and spruce as newly made beds in a hospital and at mealtimes the small table was covered with a starched white cloth, the cutlery laid correctly and white napkins in silver rings lay beside each plate. It looked far more gracious than our special Sunday tea-table at home when visitors were expected but what struck me most was that they ate tinned peaches on weekdays, an unheard of indulgence among the working-class people of our town.

Neither Mother nor Father had the time or inclination to visit the fairground amusements but as the Clarksons brought so much trade to the shop I found it easy to extract money from my parents to spend at the fair and became a regular Friday- and Saturday-night visitor. I rode on the roundabouts and the cakewalk and I played 'Housey Housey' but I favoured the 'Spinner' which was a long arm, decorated with electric light bulbs, which spun round and round. Each participant stood by an electric push button and when the Spinner started to slow down the attendant exhorted everyone to press hard to encourage the Spinner to stop by them. Every week I came home with a prize but I doubt if I pressed harder than some of the strong men who had paid their threepences for a button; I doubt if luck was so often with me but I had no doubt at all that the eldest Clarkson girl, who was in charge of the stall, could control the position where the Spinner came to rest and as she seemed to like me and someone had to win I judged she thought it might just as well be me. I was on a seesaw of anticipation as the Spinner slowed and when it stopped, pointing directly over my head, I had a wonderful time choosing which prize I should take home. Once it was a purple and gold vase; another time it was a black teapot resplendent with pink and blue and yellow daisies which Father described as being a 'bargee pot'; yet another time it was a mirror so profusely painted that you couldn't see your face in it except through a clump of bulrushes. Mother did her best to pretend that the gifts I showered on her were 'just what she wanted' but she parted with them so quickly that I began to realise she was embarrassed by them so the next time I won I chose a large tin of toffees for myself. When I opened the tin I found it was only half full so I took it back to the stall and complained. The Clarkson girl gave me what looked like an enormous box of chocolates in exchange but when I opened that it wasn't chocolate at all, it was coconut candies which tasted of soap, so I took that back too and said I'd have a bowl of goldfish but the Clarkson girl was short with me and said I'd opened the box so I must keep it. After that night she didn't smile at me so much and I didn't win nearly so often on the Spinner.

Long after my bedtime the fair carried on and as I lay in bed the lights of the Spinner were reflected on my bedroom wall. Until about ten o'clock the intervals between each spell of revolutions were brief, just long enough for the attendant to collect the money and allocate a button before starting the Spinner again but soon after ten the intervals became longer as the crowds thinned and went home leaving fewer people to be coaxed into parting with their threepences. I knew that any moment now the organ of the roundabouts would be playing its finale which with the Clarkson's Fair never varied. I snuggled down ready to sing myself to sleep with the strains of 'Good night Sweetheart'.

. . . . .

Sunday activities in winter were unvaryingly dull; after breakfast I had to face the two most hated chores of my week which were turning the handle of the grindstone while Father sharpened all the shop knives and stirring a basin of flour and water for Mother until all the lumps had disappeared. Of the two tasks I preferred the grindstone simply because I was with Father but Mother threatened there would be no gravy for dinner if I didn't do the stirring and as Father and

I believed that gravy was to Sunday dinner as juice is to an orange I sat at my task until the lumps yielded either to my stirring or my glowering looks.

Summer Sundays were far less dull. Usually my first chore after breakfast was to go down to Aunty Polly's to buy twopennyworth of mint from her garden for the sauce for dinner and though when I returned there was still the grindstone and the gravy to attend to quite frequently there were other more enjoyable things than Sunday school to look forward to in the afternoon. We might only be going to the local park to hear the band play but there were Sundays when we could sail on a steamer from Eastham along the canal and into the Mersey through the locks where the steamer sank terrifyingly low beneath the high dank walls. On other Sundays we might go to tea with some friends of Mother's at Stanlow Point which meant we had to be rowed there and back by boat and while you were there you could pretend you were on a remote island. There were also the charabanc trips on which I used to accompany Mother. It was the cycle-shop-cum-garage proprietor who ran the charabancs, two big ones which were christened 'Darby' and 'Joan' and a smaller one known as 'Baby Joan'. They were open to the weather with only a hood to pull over in case of rain but, undeterred, the townsfolk who could afford the fare packed themselves in jubilantly and from the moment they had settled in their seats to the moment they returned, their pallid faces reddened by wind and sun and beer, they sang and cheered and waved hands, handkerchiefs, hats and scarves at every passer-by they encountered. The charabancs, having names, became personalities in their own right and people spoke of going on a trip with 'Darby' or with 'Joan' and once when 'Baby Joan' disgraced herself by breaking down on a journey so that the driver had to poke about in her engine the word went round the town that 'the driver had to stop halfway to change one of "Baby Joan's" napkins'.

12

Shortly before my ninth birthday I announced to my
parents that I wished to forsake the Wesleyan chapel and go
to Sunday school and services at the Church of England.
Father was so surprised he seemed temporarily bereft of
speech, but Mother immediately came back with the reply
that I would go where I was sent and that would continue
to be the Wesleyan chapel. I argued sullenly that I hated

the Wesleyan chapel; I hated its Sunday school and even more than either I hated the lady superintendent. The superintendent was a majestic figure with purple blotches on her neck which she tried to hide beneath an inadequate fur tippet, and smouldering grey eyes which, from beneath the cover of her broad-brimmed hat, raked the rows of children like a marksman selecting an individual target.

'You can still go to the Wesleyans,' reiterated Mother.

'Well, I'm not going next Sunday. Not straight after my birthday,' I said with pleading defiance.

'All right,' she conceded. 'You needn't go next Sunday.'

Sunday-school birthdays were loathsome and mortifying. Your name was called out and you had to go and stand in front of the superintendent, facing the other children as the organist played the number of years of your age in notes on the organ and the children counted on their fingers. The organist went on to play 'Happy birthday' and all the time the superintendent stood resting her hands in blessing on your head. Her hands were fat and hot and heavy and on my last birthday she had pressed home her blessing so hard that my hat had come down over my eyes until I couldn't see what was happening. The more I fidgeted the harder she pressed and when I got home Mother upbraided me for being careless with my new hat because the crown was dished in.

Having gained a respite from Sunday school for one week I was more determined than ever to wear down my parents' resistance to my transition from chapel to church and that same evening while Mother was out at a whist drive and Father was catching up on some filing I sat at the table learning a collect from a scruffy prayer book lent to me by Cora whose family were nominally church members. Father looked over my shoulder and asked what I was doing.

'Learning my Sunday school collect,' I replied, and felt my insides cringing in anticipation of a sharp or derisive rebuke.

'You don't learn collects at the Wesleyan Sunday school,' he said shortly.

'I don't learn anything at the Wesleyan Sunday school,' I returned, knowing this was my best approach with him. 'Every week it's the same. We sing "Jesus bids us shine" and "Count the pennies dropping" and then she tells us about Moses in the bulrushes or Samuel in the temple. I'm sick of Moses and Samuel!' I cried.

'I don't suppose she knows any other stories,' admitted Father with a chuckle edging his voice. 'But all the same if your mother insists you're going to chapel Sunday school then you mustn't argue.'

But I would not give in without a fight and screwing up my courage I went to call on the vicar. The vicarage lay at the end of a long sweep of driveway overlooked by tall trees a-flutter with rooks like charred paper from a bonfire. Timidly I climbed the whitened steps and thudded the stiff black knocker against the studded door. The vicar himself opened the door and greeted me with a such big smile I thought for a moment he was laughing at me. He was very beautiful with black curly hair and eyes that were like looking up at a blue sky through leafy trees.

'Good morning,' he said. 'I don't know your name do I?' His voice skidded up and down like a knife on steel. I struggled to find my own voice.

'I want to start coming to church instead of the Wesleyan chapel,' I told him, 'and my parents won't allow me to.'

The vicar raised black eyebrows that were as dishevelled as the rooks' nests. 'Come inside a moment and we'll have a little chat,' he replied.

In his study he asked me who I was and where I lived and why I so much wanted to go to church. I told him, although I could give him no better reason for wanting to change other than that I liked the stained-glass windows in church.

'And how can I help you?' he asked.

'If you spoke to my parents?' I hazarded. 'Maybe they wouldn't say no to you.'

He made a doubtful grimace. 'I don't really know if I should,' he murmured. 'They're Welseyan Methodists you say and I don't believe I've ever met them. How d'you suppose I could get in touch with them?'

I took a deep breath. What I was going to suggest was both cheeky and treacherous. 'They have a shop,' I began, and told him all about Father and Mother and the shop. 'And if you could go and buy something from them they'll have to talk to you and you could ask them if I could come to your church,' I finished up.

'Well!' ejaculated the vicar, and smiled again his big wide smile and this time I was certain he was laughing at me. He got up. 'Leave me to think it over and I'll see what can be done,' he promised as he ushered me towards the door. I went home singing a hymn under my breath.

Two days later when I got home from school Mother greeted me with mock exasperation. 'That vicar from the church has been in the shop today and he asked if you could go to his church. Have you been getting at him?'

I admitted I had mentioned it when I saw him at school but did not disclose I had actually called at the vicarage.

'Are you going to let me go to church?' I asked demurely.

'I suppose so,' said Mother grudgingly. 'But remember if there's any sulking or tantrums about going to Sunday school like there's been lately you'll just have to go back to the chapel.'

'There won't be,' I assured her, and rushed out before she could make any more provisos. Wishing to know how the vicar had worked the magic, I waylaid the errand boy on his way home.

'Did you happen to see the vicar from the church in the shop today?' I enquired of him.

'Yes!' he responded eagerly. 'He came on his bike on his

way to tennis and he ordered a pound of biscuits and a dozen eggs and some other things. I had to deliver them to the vicarage and the woman in the kitchen said they'd plenty of biscuits and plenty of eggs and she didn't know what the vicar was up to buying more.' He broke off, eyeing me curiously. 'Why?' he asked. 'Is it for something special?'

'Oh, no,' I replied, turning my back on him now that I had the information. 'I was only asking.' I smiled, allowing myself without contrition to review my true reasons for wanting to belong to the church. According to Cora, its Sunday school was far more sociable and interesting and when I had visited the church with my school class I had enjoyed not only the stained-glass windows but the ritual and the carpeted aisle. The disciplined choir in cassocks and surplices were a far more agreeable spectacle than that provided by the chapel choir with its medley of Sunday-best outfits. Also the church choir was exclusively male with a large proportion of young boys who were nice to look at as well as having lovely treble voices which blended pleasingly with the tenors and baritones of the older men, whereas the chapel choir was composed of the middle-aged of both sexes who seemed to be intent on competing not only with the congregation but also with each other. Church activities were more exciting too, with annual 'treats' to which admission was free so long as one attended Sunday school regularly and learned one's collects. Admittedly the chapel had an annual 'treat' but it was usually nothing more alluring than a picnic and sports day on some farmer's field within easy walking distance to save the cost of transportation. I disliked group sports and I knew from experience that when the picnic buns and lemonade were produced hosts of sharp-elbowed, famished boys descended on the tables like sandhoppers on seaweed and the only buns the girls saw were the half-eaten, discarded ones the boys threw at them. In any case it always rained for the chapel 'treats' while those organised by the church seemed to be blessed with sunshine.

So I joined the church and never again was there any need for Mother to harry me either to go to Sunday school or service. I was able to join their charabanc trips to the seaside which, except for the 'free refreshments', were an exhilarating experience from the moment we packed into the fleet of charabancs until the moment we were decanted, sandy and sunburned, at the end of a long day. Despite the efforts and predictions of the organisers the refreshments were always inadequate, but at least there were shops where we could buy ice-cream and sweets to fill the empty spaces left in our stomachs by the meal of cold, urn tea and slices of stale bread that might have been briefly wiped with a margarine wrapper. There were other things we could spend our money on, such as the little hand-propelled paddle boats on the pool and a splendid fairground which boasted more adventurous amusements than we ever saw at home. We could shriek hysterically as we rode the scenic railway; un-nerve ourselves for days by a trip on the 'Ghost Train' and make ourselves weak with laughter in the 'Hall of Mirrors'. We could visit sideshows too where the indiarubber man shared a booth with a dwarf and a fat lady. The indiarubber man could stretch the skin of his chest until it covered his face; the dwarf was an incredibly tiny lady, swathed in black velvet and ropes of pearls; the astoundingly fat lady proudly declaimed that she was only seventeen, weighed twenty-one stone and could not even put on her own shoes. As I considered my own mother a fat lady I told her about the phenomenon I'd seen, but Mother was sceptical. She said the lady had been seventeen ten years previously when she herself had visited the fair and that she believed much of the fat was padding since when the indiarubber man had put his arm around her he'd left an indentation.

The church also gave a Christmas party for which the

143

catering was undertaken by a local firm with the Sunday school teachers acting as waitresses. This was so much of a banquet that many children took folded paper bags tucked into a pocket which they filled with food before they started to eat themselves. Some children even took baskets, hiding them under the table until they were full and then passing them secretly to an accomplice, usually an older relative stationed outside the hall. One or two of the Sunday school teachers were cross if they discovered children appropriating food in this way because they themselves had paper bags and baskets handy in the cloakroom which they hoped to fill when the tables were cleared.

.   .   .   .

Although Christmas celebrations were confined to the two weeks of the festival, preparations behind the scenes in the shop began several weeks earlier. Father bought in extra dried fruit in good time for people to bake their cakes and despite all the extra sieving and cleaning it meant for me my task was made less tedious by knowing I was doing something connected with all the fun and glamour of Christmas. Mother made mincemeat in a huge earthenware crock where it was left to mature for a month before it was ready for sale to customers who brought their own jars. It was wonderful mincemeat and I used to have permanent diarrhoea during that month because I could never pass the crock without stealing a spoonful. It was about three weeks before Christmas that the specialities began to arrive: iced and decorated cakes; stuffed dates; candied fruits; boxes of fancy biscuits and sweets; sugared fancies; mixed nuts and valencia raisins. I needed neither the calendar nor the displays of tinsel and decorations in the shops to tell me Christmas was approaching. I could smell its all-pervading smell, rich and spicy and appetite-pricking.

As soon as the schools broke up for the holiday—even before they banded themselves together to go carol-singing—the children could be seen dancing eager attendance on greengrocers' shops, begging or buying two wooden hoops off fruit barrels to make their 'Christmas bush' which for most families was the substitute for a Christmas tree. The 'bush' was achieved by inserting one hoop through the other at right angles and decorating it with tissue paper of different hues, cut into loops and with strands of tinsel. On Christmas Eve the bush was bedecked with baubles, small trinkets, sugar fancies, foil-wrapped neapolitans, apples and oranges, just as a tree would be, but then it was hung from the ceiling where, if the room were sufficiently airy, it provided a slowly revolving orb of colourful splendour.

Aunty Lizzie, who with her husband, Uncle Joe, shared Granny's home, was a gifted Christmas bush decorator and while other people rushed to trim their bushes last thing on Christmas Eve she was happy to spend several nights embellishing her own bush. First she collected as many different-coloured tissues as the shops could provide and after skilful cutting and ruching she attached the resulting frills to the hoops until she had achieved four miniature rainbows flamboyant enough to bring squeals of appreciation from visiting children. Both Aunty Lizzie and Granny loved Christmas and everything connected with the festival and though Uncle Joe was often on short time prior to the holiday, which meant they were short of money, they always contrived to bake dozens of mince pies and cakes and tarts in readiness for the family gathering on Christmas night.

Every year after Gran's party was over the family used to say to one another that there mustn't be another party next year. It was getting too much for Gran, they said. But every year when it came towards the end of November Aunty Lizzie announced, 'Gran says you're to make sure and come to the party at Christmas', and we always did make sure and though Mother complained to Father when we got home that the parties were a fearful strain I always enjoyed myself immensely. One year, however, in early November Gran became ill. I thought I detected a note of satisfaction in Mother's voice when she told Father: 'It means there'll be no party this year.'

Father smiled obliquely. 'She'll get better in time for Christmas or die in the attempt,' he prophesied.

'I'll be glad of a quiet Christmas,' sighed Mother.

I felt dejected. Christmas at home was already too quiet for me and I could not imagine what it would be like without Gran's party. I willed her to recover in record time and pestered Aunty Lizzie to know if I could do anything to help. At last word came that Gran was able to get up, but with only two weeks to go to Christmas she was still having to rest for the greater part of the day.

When Aunty Lizzie came into the shop Mother said: 'You'll be relieved there's to be no party this year, I'm sure. It must make a lot of work for you.'

'We're having a party,' responded Aunty Lizzie with a triumphant gleam in her eye. 'Gran said so this morning.'

'She never did!' gasped Mother.

'She did,' affirmed Aunty Lizzie. 'She said it might be her last Christmas but she wants it to be a merry one.'

'But the work!' argued Mother.

'Oh, she's going to trust me to do all the cooking,' replied Aunty Lizzie. 'She says so long as she can watch people enjoying themselves she's happy.'

Mother looked discomfited. She had convinced herself that this year she would have the quiet Christmas she yearned for and now it seemed Gran was going to be stubborn enough to deprive her of her rest. 'Well, we shan't come!' she exclaimed after a moment's hesitation. 'That means there'll be three less for you to have to cope with.'

I don't think Mother saw me glowering at her.

'She won't like that,' asserted Aunty Lizzie, who possibly suspected the reason for Mother's self-sacrifice. 'Anyway, what about Chipcart?'

'I'll come,' I piped up.

Mother gave me a quelling look. 'Chipcart can come perhaps but we shall stay at home. We couldn't bear to think we're putting a strain on you or on Gran so soon after her illness.' Mother sounded so virtuous I was almost taken in by her words and wondered, briefly, if I too ought to decline the invitation for Gran's sake.

It was again Aunty Lizzie who brought Granny's terse comment on Mother's apparent wish to defect from the annual family gatherings. 'If you don't want to come say so but if I'm well enough to ask you I'm well enough for you to come.'

'Well, I don't know whatever next,' said Mother exasperatedly. 'I suppose we'll have to humour her.'

As we had done every year since I could remember we set out in the chill dusk of Christmas day to walk to Gran's house and as always I ran ahead eager to catch the first glimpse of the lighted windows of the parlour which signified that some of the family had already arrived. One knock and the door was opened by Gran herself, paler and shakier but with her face already crinkled in a radiant smile. While we embraced and wished one another a Merry Christmas and Aunty Lizzie took our coats and Father popped his walking stick into the decorated pottery holder the little Kelly lamp flickered as if nervous at the unaccustomed activity. We went into the kitchen where the big table was already set for tea and children were occupying the long sofa which had been pulled up to the table because there were not enough chairs for everyone. Squeezing in between the other children was for me part of the ritual of the feast, as was unfolding the poppy-flowered paper serviette and putting it beneath my plate in case I dropped crumbs on the starched white cloth.

Gran's kitchen was a splendid place for parties, so bright and cheerful it seemed as if the colour and spirit of Christmas lingered there throughout the year. The big stove was, in winter or summer, aglow with the reflection of busy flames; the rosebud-patterned china on the alcove shelves was always lustrous and the red paisley-patterned cushions and covers reminded one of the colour of Santa Claus's cloak. The walls were patterned too and hung with ornaments: a white china cornucopia; a red glass half-yard of ale that looked like an outsize pipe; a yellow glass germ stick that resembled a long piece of barley sugar and had to be wiped clean of germs every day; pearl inlaid trays depicting scenes of Japanese life, and a glass dome that contained shells and coloured seaweeds from some tropical country. There were pictures too, of children crossing a farmyard and being chased by geese; of Lord Roberts, his uniform brimful of medals, and there was a framed collection of hand-embroidered valentines which Gran had collected during the Boer War and which I loved to be allowed to admire at close quarters.

When tea was over the trinkets and sweets from the Christmas bush were distributed among the children; the women washed dishes in the back kitchen and the men produced pipes and cigarettes and lit them with spills ignited in the fire. There was always a plentiful supply of spills on the hob at Granny's, thanks to Uncle Joe who spent his Sunday mornings cutting them, and except for lighting the fire each day matches were never used. Someone noticed that Granny was becoming agitated because, she said, the gas was flaring above the mantle and there was a tetchy moment while Uncle Joe, who was very short-sighted, stood on a chair and adjusted the light by pulling first one chain and then the other in compliance with the many directions he received. There was gaslight in only the kitchen at Granny's and as she was still inclined to regard it with awe it was usually turned low for safety.

As soon as the women had finished the dishes and taken off their borrowed aprons everyone, except Granny, who was too frail, and Aunty Lizzie, who was too busy, joined in games like 'Hunt the Slipper', 'Consequences', and 'Passing the Ring'. Ginger wine was produced for the children and a bottle of port wine for the adults, which no doubt helped to increase the fervour of their voices when the brass lantern clock showed a quarter to nine and we all moved into the parlour for a sing-song round the harmonium. The Christmas party always ended with a sing-song and the sing-song always ended with Granny's favourite hymn; old and young joined in singing 'The day Thou gavest, Lord, is ended' to the audience of glass pigs on the mantelpiece, while Granny relaxed in her armchair, nodding and smiling on us with pride and satisfaction.

We put on our outdoor clothes, said our goodbyes and went out into the frost-cold, silent street. Father set a jaunty pace for the walk home to which I hummed one of the songs we had been singing earlier.

As soon as we reached our own house Mother went straight to the living room and sagged into her chair.

'I'm jiggered,' she complained. 'I felt roasted all evening.'

'It does get hot,' agreed Father.

'Well, I hope there won't be a party next year, that's all,' she said fretfully.

Father looked at her steadily for a moment and then turned away. 'There's only one way there won't be a party,' he said pointedly, 'and after all, she's your mother.'

13

The shop brought me into contact with a fascinating variety of people and accents I had never come across before. Travellers came competing for business in refined Lancashire, emphatic Yorkshire and broad Scottish and I used to amuse Father by mimicking them and their ready, ingratiating laughter. Invariably they tried to be charming to me, although I made no secret of the fact that I despised them all. 'Is this your little girl?' they used to ask Father when I appeared, and when Father acknowledged me they made flattering remarks which made me squirm because I knew they were as spurious as those my parents felt compelled to bestow on some of the little horrors our customers introduced as their progeny.

Assisting the errand boys in their deliveries also helped me to meet many different people, though there were one or two houses where I was banned from visiting no matter how overworked the errand boys might be. One house was that of Mrs James, a plump and pretty widow who Father always described as 'starving her belly to clothe her back'. She had a selection of male visitors and on Saturday nights used to come into the shop with a long evening gown trailing beneath her coat, high-heeled dance slippers tucked under her arm, her face coated with powder and rouge and reeking of scent. On Monday mornings she'd be in wearing an old skirt and jersey, half covered by a loose hip-length coat for which the local term was a 'bum-starver', and buying odd pieces of bacon, cracked eggs and broken biscuits. I could never understand why my parents disapproved so strongly of Mrs James. To me she was a very glamorous person, and when one day there was a message to be delivered to her and no one but myself available I begged to be allowed to go.

'All right,' said Father, relenting. 'But make sure you just hand over the goods and don't go inside.'

Although it was eleven o'clock in the morning Mrs James came to the door wearing a red silk dressing gown, with her face made up as if for a Saturday-night dance. A gramophone was playing jazz music and I was so intrigued that when she told me to step inside while she emptied the basket I did so readily and caught a glimpse of a wine bottle on the table and several glasses while over the back of a chair hung a pair of men's trousers. I wanted to creep in a little further, but Mrs James met me with the basket, so I didn't see if there was anyone with her, but before the door closed I heard the unmistakable sound of a man's voice.

When I got home I told Father about the gramophone and Mrs James's dressing gown and made-up face and Mother coming in at that moment listened with dismay.

'You didn't send her there,' she accused Father.

'I had to,' he replied. 'There was no one else.'

'She would have done without for me,' returned Mother tartly.

'Don't be silly,' retorted Father. 'She's a customer and she pays. Anyway, Chipcart didn't go inside, did you, Chipcart?'

'No,' I lied, deciding it was best to keep quiet about the wine bottle and the trousers, but I couldn't help wishing that my mother was more like Mrs James and that she would wear a red silk dressing gown and have the gramophone on at eleven o'clock in the morning. Mrs James seemed to get so much more fun out of life.

.   .   .   .   .

Many of our customers were the families of steelworkers who had come from the Midlands when the new steelmill was built, and their accents, though peculiar, were considered so unattractive that mimicry was forbidden. They said 'aint' instead of 'haven't' or 'am not' and they spoke of themselves as having come from 'Brum' when they meant West Bromwich and 'Up Wum' when they meant Wolverhampton. They were on the whole an uncouth, beer-swilling, whippet-racing, pigeon-fancying people who lived in a colony of cheerless streets lined with identical red brick houses built by the steel manufacturers and perhaps because of the torrid heat of the factories in which they worked they seemed to spend as much of their lives on their doorsteps as inside their homes, so that their Saturday-night squabbles were as public as a dogfight.

Every morning I used to be aroused from sleep by the steelmen going to work. Their shortest route lay past our shop and at five o'clock the silence of the morning would be broken by the first unhurried clump of clogged feet striking lonely echoes from the pavement. They came sporadically at first but as the clock ticked its way round the half-hour the noise increased steadily until by half past five it had reached its shattering metallic crescendo. I used to put the pillow over my head to try to shut out the clamour and yearned to be back at Wesley House where there had been only the howling of lost dogs to disturb my slumbers. After half past five the noise thinned, footsteps became noticeably more rapid, and interspersed by the frequent rasp of iron against the pavement as a hurrying foot skidded. By a quarter to six the street was quiet again save perhaps for the swift patter of leather-soled shoes as some late sleeper raced to beat the factory clock. It was suicidal to try to run in clogs and a minute late clocking in meant the loss of half an hour's pay, so the only course for lie-a-beds was to wear soft shoes and tuck their clogs under their arm. At six o'clock I could safely sink back into sleep again until Mother called me to get up and by this time I could witness another procession to the factory gates. This time it was the wives and daughters tripping along taking breakfast to their menfolk. They hurried past, with a saucer in a red and white polka dotted handkerchief, known as a 'red billy', slung from one hand and an enamelled can of tea from the other. It was a weekday ritual for the early-morning shift men to have their breakfast taken to them in time for eight o'clock just as it was for the 'two till ten' men to have their tea taken for six o'clock. For many of the schoolchildren it was a regular chore. I envied them because when they were late for school they had only to plead that they had to 'take breakfast' to go unpunished and similarly whatever their misdemeanours they could never be kept in after school if they had to 'take tea'. I longed to participate in what seemed to be such an important task, but as no one connected with us worked at the mills and as the rest of the populace despised the 'Up-Wummers' for the practice I realised that the opportunity was unlikely to arise. However, my chance did come. Across the street from us there lived a very charming lady, a Mrs Kenyon, for whom I used to run messages on a Saturday morning in return for a regular payment of threepence per week. Mr Kenyon worked at the mills to which his devoted wife regularly took him his meals. One Saturday Mrs Kenyon disclosed that her lodger was ill in bed and as she did not think it right to leave him alone in the house she asked me if I thought my parents would allow me to 'take breakfast' to her husband for a few days. I was delighted, but when I put the question to Mother she refused emphatically.

'There's no child of mine going to belittle themselves doing that sort of thing,' she said.

'But I want to,' I insisted. 'To see what it's like.'

Mother looked at me exasperatedly. 'I don't know what I've done to deserve à child like you,' she complained. 'You'll be telling me next you want to join the queue at the pawn shop on Monday mornings to see what that's like.'

I alternately sulked and pleaded until eventually she told me I must ask Father.

Father looked startled and I thought he too was going to refuse to let me go. 'You don't mean to tell me you really want to go with all those common children and take breakfast?' he asked incredulously.

'I do,' I replied. 'Honest and truly. Just once.'

I suspected that Father might yield because Mrs Kenyon was a Welsh woman, a compatriot of his. She was also a good customer.

'You'll never get up in time to take breakfast for eight o'clock,' he taunted me.

'I will,' I replied indignantly. 'If I promise.' We had been given a lecture on the sin of breaking promises in school the day before and I was bursting with resolution.

'All right,' Father agreed. 'If you can get up in time to have your own breakfast first and get yourself ready for half past seven you can go. Mind you,' he went on, 'getting ready means washing your neck as well as your hands and face.' I promised and asked in return for his promise to call me in good time.

'I'll call you once,' he stipulated, 'and if you don't get up then I shan't try again.' He was smiling as he said it, obviously believing that his conditions would produce the same result as a refusal. Mother came into the shop and saw my triumphant smile.

'You're not going to let her go, are you?' she asked.

'Only if she gets up at the first call,' he told her.

'You shouldn't have given in,' she chided him.

'Why not?' He grinned at her. 'It might do her good to try it.'

On Monday morning Father was astounded when I bounded out of bed the moment I heard his voice and so anxious was I not to be late that I arrived at Mrs Kenyon's house before she had finished cooking her husband's breakfast. The kettle, with a saucer for a lid, was steaming on the stove; there was bacon frying in the pan. I watched her cut a thick slice of bread, dip it in the fat and then transfer it to the warmed saucer; two rashers of bacon went on top of the bread and a second slice, equally thick and similarly dipped, was placed over it. A lightly fried egg capped the whole and then the remaining fat in the pan was poured over the egg. It seeped through the bread until the saucer was brimming. She spread a clean 'red billy' on the table, placed the saucer on it and gathering up the four corners of the handkerchief tied them in two knots to form a sling. She next put a handful of tea into the can, poured on boiling water and stirred in some condensed milk. I slid my hand through the loops of the red billy and took the can by the handle.

'Don't tilt the saucer so that the fat spills,' instructed Mrs Kenyon. 'My husband can't abide spilled fat.'

I held it gingerly as she opened the door to let me out.

'Now,' Mrs Kenyon explained. 'It won't be Mr Kenyon coming to collect his breakfast but his young mate. You'll easily pick him out because he's tall and thin with dark curly hair and a pale face, but you'll have to speak up when you see him since he doesn't know you.' I was quite sure I should have no difficulty and proudly set off for the factory. At the gates I joined the cluster of women who waited patiently to hand over their saucers and cans. At ten minutes to eight on the works clock several clogged and leather-aproned young men appeared and flicking arrogant glances of recognition at the women claimed the breakfasts they carried, slinging them on to a thin strip of steel sheet to facilitate carrying. I accosted the handsomest man among them. He was tall with dark curly hair and blue eyes. He wore a sweat cloth draped over the back of his neck and his union shirt was open over his chest, showing a 'V' of moist white skin. I was overcome with admiration for him.

'Mr Kenyon's breakfast?' I enquired.

With a barely perceptible nod he took it from me, glancing disdainfully at the dark red patch on the handkerchief where, despite my caution, the fat had seeped through. I watched him anxiously as he clumped back to the works. He had collected two or three other breakfasts at the same time and I was afraid he would spill even more of Mrs Kenyon's fat for which I should get the blame. I didn't realise that by now the fat would have congealed.

The next morning I was not quite so early at Mrs Kenyon's. 'Now, do try not to spill the fat, dear,' she instructed as she let me out. 'Mr Kenyon said it was all over the hand-kerchief yesterday.' She had promised me a shilling at the weekend for taking breakfast and I didn't want to risk having the rate cut because I spilled too much fat. My arm was cramped by the time I reached the works but despite my care there was a large dark stain again on the 'red billy'. On the third morning the sky was sullen with threatened rain.

'You'll have to take an umbrella this morning. It wouldn't do to let Mr Kenyon's breakfast get wet, would it?' It was not then raining but she hooked an umbrella over my arm and before I had gone very far the rain started. I put down the saucer and can on the pavement while I opened the umbrella and at the same time foiled a dog which had bounded out of a nearby house and looked as if it was going to demolish or defile the saucer. In fending it off with the umbrella I knocked over the can of tea. Other breakfast-carrying women giggled as they passed me with umbrellas tilted not to protect themselves but their precious burdens. With the can in one hand and the saucer in the other I could not contrive to hold the umbrella so I tucked the handle down inside my coat and let the spokes rest on my head which made it horribly uncomfortable but with half the contents of the can gone at least I did not have to be careful about the scalding hot tea splashing my legs.

It was eight o'clock when I reached the works gate and there were only two women waiting. A minute or two later a man came up and took the breakfasts from them but he paid no attention to me.

'Can you take Mr Kenyon's breakfast?' I pleaded. It was raining heavily now. The can was cold and the 'red billy' was a sodden rag. Fat had spilled on the umbrella and on my stockings and congealed into white dribbles.

'I doan work in the same shop as 'im,' the man said. 'You mun wait till 'is mate gets 'ere.'

I waited miserably and just before half past eight my Adonis appeared looking thoroughly bad-tempered.

'Yo'm late,' he greeted me. I nodded guiltily. 'What's this?' he demanded, taking the saucer and can from me.

He lifted the lid of the can and looked inside as if he was expecting to dispose of the contents into the gutter.

'I knocked it over,' I explained apologetically, 'when I tried to put up the umbrella.'

He turned slightly aside and spat abruptly. Just as abruptly my admiration for him died.

'Yo mun git 'ere a bit airlier termorrer,' he shouted at me. 'An' see as it's a breakfast when you bring it, not a muck-heap like this.'

I turned away from him, angry and disgusted, and ran all the way to school, knowing that though I should be late I'd escape punishment because of my excellent excuse. But when I smugly pleaded I'd had to 'take breakfast' the teacher raised a cynical eyebrow and admonished me for telling stories. She made me stay in after school and write out fifty times 'I must not be late'.

When Father called me next morning I turned over and went to sleep, preferring to forego my shilling than to take breakfast ever again. I felt no compunction at all for Mrs Kenyon, who would no doubt wait expectantly for my arrival, give up hope and finally hurry out with Mr Kenyon's breakfast herself. I thought it served her right for being married to a steelworker.

Pay day for most of our customers was Friday and on Friday evenings the shop was always bustling with people who had come to place or collect their weekly orders; to pay their bills or offer their excuses for not paying them; to bring rumours of threats of short time in the mills or to learn from the gossip if there was anything 'on the anvil' as they put it which might point to the possibility of jobs becoming available in the future. In the good weeks whole families came, adding a fillip to their evening by forgathering inside and outside the shop and sharing in the general conversation. The children wore their best clothes and clamoured for biscuits; the wives wore threadbare coats and fixed yearning eyes on the shelves of tinned fruits; the husbands wore archaic suits and their beaming faces were often half eclipsed by new caps which were the 'Up Wummers' first acknowledgment of relative affluence.

Friday nights were also favoured by the lascar crews of any ship which might be in port over the weekend and, intent on restocking their meagre galleys, they came intermittently in gaggling threesomes and foursomes, wearing loose cotton trousers and tunics with gay handkerchiefs knotted around their thin brown necks and soft, shuffly shoes on otherwise bare feet. The lascars were testy and suspicious and Father was relieved to discover that their purchases were mostly confined to soap and cheese since he had difficulty in interpreting their shrilly, gabbled attempts at English. When they had first presented themselves as customers he had been nonplussed by their demand for 'Fourteen wash!' and seeing his mystification each one of them had attempted to mime, gesticulate and explain, with much flashing of gold teeth, that it was fourteen bars of soap they wanted. There were many brands of soap and Father held up one at a time while the lascars shook their heads and argued vehemently with each other. Not until he produced a bar of 'Sunlight' soap did they convey their satisfaction by slapping the counter until the scales rattled. Once when the lascars came Father happened to be short of 'Sunlight' soap and suggested making up their order with 'Lifebuoy' soap which, he managed to convey to them with some difficulty, was manufactured by the same firm. The lascars muttered together doubtfully and then one of them who spoke a little more English than his mates spoke up: 'No Lifebuoy,' he said. 'Him makes Lifebuoy out of Sunlight gone bad.'

There were other ships which docked fairly regularly at the port and which were provisioned by us but then it was invariably the steward who came to place the order. The stewards were always welcomed and treated to cups of tea in the kitchen since they bought only the best quality goods and their orders were large—large enough for Father to have to borrow a handcart before the errand boy could deliver them. One evening, however, after the shop had closed there came a rattling at the door and when Father went to see who was there a man's voice announced himself as Captain Read, the skipper of a boat called the *St Helena*, and asked if he could place an order for delivery the following morning. He apologised for the lateness of the hour but said he had been placing orders for meat—he named the butcher —and for oil—he named the supplier, and this had taken rather longer than he had anticipated. Father welcomed him tepidly; Mother went into the kitchen to make tea and while Father wrote out his most impressive order I hid behind the sugar sack and watched. It was the first time I had seen a captain of a ship at close quarters and I was disappointed. I'd seen cleaner and better-dressed men collecting rags and bones. Mother brought tea and biscuits through to the shop and the man ate and drank while he carelessly ordered quantities of cheese and bacon, sugar, butter and many other groceries. After he had gone Father said dubiously: 'I thought captains of ships dressed a lot better than that fellow; he looks more like a gaberlunzie to me.'

'It depends on what sort of ship he's on,' replied Mother, who, having worked in a canteen for a time during the war, was supposed to know a lot about seamen.

'I'd have thought he was a greaser, not a skipper,' persisted Father. 'Did you see his hands? They were filthy.'

'Oh, sometimes the skippers of old tramps get themselves pretty dirty,' retorted Mother with such an assured toss of her head that I suspected she was deluding herself.

'Well, if we're going to have this order ready for delivery at eleven o'clock in the morning we'll have to start on it at six at the latest,' warned Father. 'It'll take a long time to get everything weighed out.'

'I don't mind getting up at six for an order this size,' gloated Mother. 'I'd stay up all night to do it.'

The next morning Father and Mother were hard at work when I got up and the moment the errand boy arrived he was sent to borrow the handcart. He came back with the news that the butcher had already borrowed it to take a consignment of meat to the *St Helena* and Father would have to wait until he got back. Half an hour later the oilman, looking extremely agitated, rushed into the shop.

'Did you send anything to the *St Helena* this morning?' he asked.

Father indicated the enormous order piled in front of the counter ready to be loaded into the handcart as soon as it returned. 'Not yet,' he said. 'But it's all ready.'

'There's no such ship as the *St Helena*!' the oilman burst out. 'And no such person as Captain Read. Nobody's heard of either. It's all a rotten trick.'

Father was visibly shaken. 'Are you certain?' he asked. 'Maybe she isn't docked yet.'

'She's neither docked nor expected,' asserted the oilman. 'We've been bamboozled and that's the truth of it. I sent gallons of oil and stuff down there before eight o'clock this morning and I've had to bring it all back again.' The oilman went away still shaking his head and muttering about trickery.

Father, who had been suspicious the night before, seemed as if he couldn't bear now to have his suspicions confirmed. 'We'll see what the butcher says when he comes back,' he told Mother. 'He might have found the ship all right.' But the butcher only confirmed the oilman's story. There was indeed no ship called the *St Helena* anywhere near the port and among all the captains who called at the docks no one had heard of a Captain Read.

With his mouth set in a bitter line Father started to stow the carefully weighed-out goods back on to shelves or into the storeroom. 'I told you I thought he was too dirty to be a captain,' he snapped accusingly at Mother.

'At least we haven't had the trouble of delivering the stuff before we found out,' replied Mother meekly.

Father was taking the greaseproof paper off one of two seven-pound packs of butter the pseudo skipper had ordered. 'Why d'you think he did it?' he mused in a puzzled voice. 'He couldn't have expected to get anything out of it and he didn't try to borrow money or anything.'

'He got tea and biscuits,' responded Mother. 'And I expect he got something from the oilman's wife and from the butcher's wife. All in all he probably got a good supper out of us.'

'Aye,' said Father, 'and he probably enjoyed himself more than if he'd gone to the workhouse for it.'

.   .   .   .   .

On Saturday nights the 'boaties', as we called the people from the canal barges, surged colourfully into town, each family making its own insulated procession and walking with eyes fixed straight ahead. The women wore calf-length buttoned boots, full plaid skirts covered with stiff white aprons, shawls and men's caps. The men wore narrow moleskin trousers, serge jackets and uniform peaked caps and both sexes sported ear-rings and robust, fancy-buckled leather belts. The belts looked both efficient and menacing. It was reputed that when a boatie child misbehaved the fingers of their parents always strayed to the region of their belts and Fran had told me that when she had witnessed some men boaties fighting outside their pub the women had quickly thrown off their shawls, unbuckled their belts and started to thwack one another as an accompaniment to the fisticuffs of their menfolk.

They were a tough, fearless race, reserving their quarrels to themselves on the whole and though the term 'boatie' or even 'bargee' was uttered by the townspeople much as an epithet, they were proud and hardworking; they might haggle exasperatingly over a farthing yet never demean themselves by owing one. Father didn't much care for the boaties coming into the shop, since not only did they take up so much space with their wide skirts, enormous shopping baskets and attendant crews of children, but so apprehensive were other customers about coming into contact with them that they were inclined to pass by when they saw them. Fortunately, however, the boaties usually arrived in the slack teatime hour so that they could finish shopping in time for the evening opening of the pubs and if I was at home I loved to be in the shop when they came. They were almost the only people who bought old-fashioned things like the strong blue mottled scrubbing soap which they had cut into lengths to fit their baskets; rottenstone for brass cleaning; they insisted on the broken starch that looked like pieces of white macaroni though it had long been superseded for the rest of our customers by the much advertised refined starch that came in measured packets, and it was the boaties too who steadfastly refused to accept tinned treacle instead of the 'loose molasses' from the barrel for which they brought their own jars or jugs. As soon as I saw a boatie woman produce an empty jar from her cloth-covered basket my mouth started to water. Everyone else disliked the sticky job of getting molasses because it meant they had to stop and wash their hands afterwards, but I was only too eager to take the jar out to the storeroom, turn on the tap of the barrel and watch the varnish-brown runnel filling the jar, knowing that when the tap was turned off there would be dribbles I could catch on my finger. There was no need to wash my hands after getting molasses. I always licked them clean.

At the back of Fran's home there was a paddock and a

large shed where, over the weekend, the boaties grazed or housed the horses which pulled their barges and as it was often the boatie children who tended the horses we got to know one of them reasonably well. Her name was Connie and unlike the other boatie children of whom we were both fearful and contemptuous she was a gentle quiet girl who liked to collect flowers and grasses to paint and made up poetry which she recited to us. We had even sneaked off to a service at the Mission chapel with Connie and joined lustily with the boatie congregation singing such hymns as 'Throw out the Lifeline' and 'I'm steering my boat to Heaven'.

Since Fran's mother had continued to be a customer at the shop I was no longer flatly forbidden to visit her home, only discouraged from doing so, which resulted in my going there whenever the opportunity arose. One Saturday evening we were sitting in Fran's bedroom eating 'tiger nuts' which I was forbidden to eat at home because Father said they were rat muck dipped in sugar, which in fact they looked like. We were watching some boaties dancing outside the pub to the music of an itinerant barrel-organ when we spotted Connie and her brother being handed the shopping basket by their parents and instructed to carry it the rest of the way down to the boat, leaving their parents to join in the fun. Seeing the two children going off on their own Fran and I set off in pursuit. Connie did not seem overpleased to see us and her brother positively glowered at us, but we were not deterred and fell in a pace or two behind them. At the canal bank we waited while brother and sister lugged the heavy basket aboard and took it into the cabin. It was some time before Connie reappeared and spoke to us.

'I've got to mind the boat,' she called.

Fran dug her elbow into my side. 'Can we come on board?' she called back daringly.

I was aghast. We weren't supposed even to talk to a boatie, never mind set foot on a barge.

Connie looked startled and disappeared into the cabin. When she emerged I was thankful to see she was shaking her head in an emphatic negative.

'Just for a minute,' Fran coaxed. 'We won't tell.'

Connie poked her head into the cabin and we could hear her arguing with her brother. She stood up, scrutinising the other moored barges, and then motioned us to join her.

'No,' I started to protest, but Fran was already stepping aboard and I followed. Through the swing doors we were confronted by such a tiny space I doubted if there was room to sit down and yet as I wondered I realised that there was no lack of all the necessary equipment that makes a home. It was the neatness and compactness that staggered me. There was an open range with a bright fire burning and two kettles on the hob; there was a table; bunks to sit on and shelves crowded with crockery and kitchen utensils; there was even room for ornaments like china dogs and vases. Everything that could be decorated was painted with flowers and leaves and birds in a galaxy of colours and though Connie claimed to have done much of it herself, her brother, who sat sulkily whittling away at a piece of wood that was beginning to resemble a spoon, interpolated that most of it had been painted by their grandfather. Fran and I sat quietly for a few minutes taking it all in and listening to the plop of water rats into the canal.

'D'you think we could have a cup of tea?' Connie enquired of her brother.

He muttered something about taking the blame if they were found out and Connie looked worried. After a few moments, however, she put some tea from a colourful caddy into an equally colourful teapot. She tilted one of the steaming kettles and the water that came out looked as if it too had been mixed with a little paint. Connie pushed full mugs along to us and the tea tasted strong and sweet.

Fran asked suddenly: 'Do you wash yourselves in canal water?'

'Of course,' replied Connie, confirming one of the sneering imputations we had heard against boaties. The canal was not noted for cleanliness. Any day you could walk along the bank and see dead animals floating in it, while the effluent discharged continuously from some of the canalside factories looked far from hygienic.

I, seeing no tap aboard and recollecting that I'd never noticed a fresh-water tap along the canalside, asked where they got their drinking water.

'The same,' asserted Connie with some surprise. She saw my expression. 'There's nothing wrong with it. It keeps us healthy and anyway that's good tea, isn't it?'

It had been but it wasn't any longer.

Fran put down her cup and looking at it with distaste slid it away from her.

'But it's dirty, filthy water in the canal,' she expostulated.

'Just here it is,' conceded Connie. 'But we fill our buckets when we get further up the canal by the farmlands. It's nice and clean there.'

I thought again of the dead animals which appeared to me to travel along the canal at much the same rate as the barges and I looked with loathing at my half-empty mug. I thought I was going to be sick.

Connie said: 'You'll have to go now. Somebody might catch us.' She picked up the mugs and going out emptied the slops over the side.

'I'll empty the teapot,' said Fran helpfully as Connie picked up a bucket. She dashed to the side, tipped up the teapot and Connie let out an agonised yell as there was a 'plop' and the lid of the pot fell into the canal. Her face went white with fear and Fran's hand went to her mouth in a gesture of horror. I was standing at the entrance to the cabin when I was pushed roughly out of the way by Connie's brother. As he took in what had happened his own face went white and then, snatching the pot from Fran, he attacked first her and then me, punching, pushing, pulling our hair and swearing at us in a low savage voice.

Fran and I jumped off the barge and ran as fast as we could with Connie's brother not far behind us hurling missiles and imprecations. We dared not seek the safety of the pub, since Connie's father was likely to be there, and continued running until we had nearly reached my own home.

'Her father!' gasped Fran. 'He's ever such a bully. He'll chase us with his belt and thrash us.'

I started to cry. 'We'll be found out about going on a barge and knowing Connie,' I wailed, imagining the severity of the punishment I should get from my parents.

'I'm going to creep back home and wash the dishes for my mother,' said Fran, brightening. 'She won't say anything then even if she does find out.'

I went home, dreading they might have heard of my escapade already, but nothing was said and I went to bed still feeling thoroughly miserable and frightened. In the night I was sick.

'What did you have to eat at Fran's that's made you sick?' Mother demanded to know. I remembered the tiger nuts but I didn't mention them. 'Or drink?' persisted Mother. 'It could have been something you drank.'

Until that moment I had forgotten the canal-water tea and I felt sick again as the memory of it assailed me.

'I had some dandelion and burdock,' I admitted cautiously.

Mother looked at me exasperatedly. 'It's never made you sick before,' she grumbled.

Our visit to the barge was never discovered so far as Fran and I knew and whatever happened about the loss of the teapot lid no repercussions ever reached our ears. It was three weeks later before we caught a glimpse of Connie but she never spoke to us again.

14

When the General Strike and the years of depression came it was a disastrous time for customers and tradespeople, and the conventional greeting between housewives was no longer 'Good morning' or 'Good evening' or even 'Hello', but 'Is he working?' and between men it was 'Are you working?'. All too often the answer was a hopeless 'Not yet'. Debts accumulated, food prices were slashed and still people looked for cheaper and cheaper food. Greengrocers were offering 'a week's fruit and vegetables for a shilling' and were outdone by competitors who offered 'a week's fruit and vegetables for a shilling with a penny back'. Quasi jam could be bought for sixpence a two-pound jar; Cheshire cheese sold at sixpence a pound, and eggs, imported from China, retailed at only a few pence per dozen. Father bought a crate of Chinese eggs in readiness for Shrove Tuesday when there was always an extra demand for eggs for pancakes. They were small and their shells had a greenish tinge and though Father himself didn't fancy eating them because he said Chinese hens scratched in graveyards for their sustenance, they sold to customers who were glad to be able to buy eggs so cheaply. Father had taken the consignment with the proviso that bad ones would be credited by the wholesaler, who in turn imposed the condition that any rejects must first be inspected by their traveller. Father soon realised his mistake. There were many bad eggs in the consignment and when customers brought them back to be exchanged the eggs were tipped into a bucket to await the traveller. As he called only once a week our backyard was stinking like a blocked sewer before the contents of the bucket could be disposed of and Father never dealt in Chinese eggs again.

By this time he had bought the house next door which provided us with plenty of living space. The former living room behind the shop became a combined store and office and the kitchen became a sort of cookhouse where 'funeral hams' were boiled in the big copper and where a large mincing machine was installed for mincing odd scraps of bacon to be made into brawn and sausages. Father took me with him to Liverpool when he went to buy the sausage skins from a frowsy warehouse where clogged and overalled women clumped over the dank stone floor fetching and carrying overfull buckets of gruesome entrails. One of the women put down a bucket overflowing with something I didn't dare look at too closely to attend to us and when Father asked for sausage skins she led us to a row of sturdy oak barrels packed tight with dried and salted skins that looked like nests of anaemic worms. She weighed out several pounds but though she wrapped them well in several sheets of paper I could still smell them all the way home. Before they could be used the sausage skins had to be fixed to the cold water tap so that the water ran through them, cleaning them of salt and at the same time swelling them. It was fascinating to watch the skins inflating and assuming their long, semi-transparent tube shape as they were swilled. Once they were ready one end of the skin was fixed to a special gadget on the mincer and as the handle was turned the minced meat was forced into the skin until there was a sausage as long as a skipping rope ready to be taken off the mincer and twisted into links. As they were composed largely of left-over ends of bacon and the skins were cheap our sausages could be sold for about sixpence a pound which, so long as there was no costing of the labour involved, was mainly profit. Father used to sing as he churned away at the handle of the mincing machine as if he was churning out pound notes and if a tramp called begging for food Mother would fry up some sausages for him. When a group of hungry, out-of-work Welsh miners came, singing for pennies in the street, Father sent me out with a bag of sausages and brawn sandwiches and, because he was half Welsh himself and felt desperately sorry for the miners, there was a half-crown to give them too. There were tears in the eyes of the miner who took the food and money from me and in my innocence I thought they must be singing a very sad song.

Another of Father's enterprises was to pack our own peas and tea which would give a better profit margin and enable us to compete with the bulk buying of the multiple stores and the 'divi' offered by the Co-operative Society. We had a lovely time choosing packets and brand names from the range sent by the paper merchants and eventually for the peas we chose a shiny, bright red carton with a picture of a large yellow wicker basket full of plump green peas. Father decided on the name 'Golden Basket' and when the cartons arrived the three of us were busy weighing and packing. Although exactly the same peas from the identical sack could be bought loose for threepence a pound the colourful packet and the fact that we gave a halfpenny for each packet returned ensured that 'Golden Basket' sold even better at fourpence halfpenny for fourteen ounces. Also, when buying loose peas a customer expected to have to soak them with a piece of washing soda added to the water, whereas the instructions on our cartons read: 'Soak the peas overnight along with one of the enclosed special tablets'. The 'special tablet' added glamour to the pack, even though it was only compressed soda, and customers refused to buy the 'rotten old loose peas'. This made Father beam happily, since the loose peas gave him a profit of less than a halfpenny a pound whereas 'Golden Basket', even after paying for the packet and the tablets and giving a halfpenny back, still showed a profit of a penny a pound, a large profit for those days when a halfpenny was the difference between the wholesale and retail price of two pounds of sugar and out of that the retailer had to provide the bag and the time and labour of weighing out.

Our packed tea we called 'Calcutta Brand' and because Father favoured red above all other colours for display purposes he again chose red packets with blue seals. As with the peas, customers could buy the same tea loose at twopence a quarter less than 'Calcutta Brand' but with the attraction of a halfpenny for each empty packet they were easily able to convince themselves that the packed tea was superior and soon there was so little demand for loose tea Father was able to say it was no longer worth stocking.

The extra work of sausage- and brawn-making, tea- and pea-packing was a fearful strain on my parents, but during those stark days there were many who would have been glad of the chance to work equally hard, so Father and Mother carried on striving for the standard of living they dreamed of. They were now paying for my education plus books, uniform, and the daily rail fares to and from school; they employed a girl to do the books and another girl to help in the house and counting two errand boys that made four strangers around the house and shop. To Mother that meant four aliens sharing our lavatory and she began agitating for a bathroom and lavatory to be installed inside the house for our own private use. Although with the two houses we now had two outside W.C.s Mother was far from satisfied. She was faddish about some things and our lavatory was one of them. Unlike the neighbours, we always kept our yard door bolted in case some hawker or gypsy woman who, feeling a need to relieve herself, would open the nearest yard door and nip in before anyone could stop her. Admittedly some of the more polite ones came to the house door and asked if they might use the W.C., in which case I had been trained to say, 'Sorry, it's occupied at the moment and he'll be a long time.' I had to say 'he' because it was unthinkable that a woman should take a long time on the lavatory.

Father, willingly yielding to Mother's persuasions, sent for the plumber and within a few days the work was commenced. To have an inside lavatory was considered a status symbol and Father had promised me I should be the first one to use it. I hung around the house all day, but just before Father had predicted the lavatory would be finished I saw the plumber approaching him with a worried look on his face. He had almost finished installing the lavatory, he said, but unfortunately he had just dropped his heavy hammer down into the pan and the whole thing had shattered. Father was both disappointed and angry, but there was nothing he could do save buy a new lavatory pan which arrived the following day with a much deflated plumber in attendance. This time we heard the crash of the hammer succeeded by the clatter of porcelain before the plumber, shrivelled with apology, came to confess that inconceivably the same accident had again happened. Father chided him bitterly, but as he and the plumber were old friends he ordered yet another lavatory pan and the same plumber arrived to do the job. This time, however, Father wasn't going to risk an accident. At that time our errand boy was Hugo, a small timid boy who crackled every winter because of the goose-grease and brown paper plasters he wore under his vest for his weak chest. He had large blue eyes which nearly popped out of his head when he was afraid of anything, which was fairly often. When he had come to us it was his first experience of electricity and he found it quite terrifying. If he was asked to put on a switch his eyes would pop, he would lift his right arm tentatively, flick the switch and immediately grab the wrist with his left hand, doubling up and waiting for the shock he was sure would come. When Father gave him instructions to sit on the lavatory until it was finally installed and the tools taken safely out of the way Hugo's eyes looked like miniature balloons.

'What if he drops the hammer on me?' he asked shrilly.

'Catch it, you silly fool,' said Father, and as both lavatory and Hugo were intact when the plumber left we had to assume that he did.

As I grew older more and more jobs were found for me to do in the shop and since I was now attending Secondary School to and from which I had to travel each day by train my life was crammed with work. It was deliberate policy on my parents' part to fully occupy my evenings so that I was kept 'off the streets' and, more important still, from contact with boys, for though they had not hesitated to send me to a co-educational school friendships with boys outside school hours were strictly forbidden. I dared not be seen even talking

173

to a boy and the only excuse I could make to get out in an evening was to say I had forgotten one of my textbooks and could not do my homework unless I borrowed one from a school-mate. As a result of so much confinement I grew pale and anaemic; the excellent school reports I had been bringing home showed my position in the form declining from third to twenty-fifth, while the 'teacher's remarks', hitherto complimentary and encouraging, began to make such observations as 'Seems to have lost interest in her work' and 'Very disappointing result'. Father grew angrier and angrier and at last wrote to the headmaster asking if I misbehaved at school to merit such results. The headmaster replied giving his opinion that it was my health Father should be worrying about, not my work, and as a result the doctor was immediately called in. In addition to ordering me to take several different medicines, pills and emulsions the doctor said I needed a holiday and plenty of fresh air and to my great delight I was packed off to the country for a month. When I returned instead of finding me jobs in the shop Father gave me outdoor work to do. I was considered responsible enough to deliver the 'Blackbirds', my father's euphemism for bottles of Worthington, to staunch chapel folk who though they liked a drink could neither be seen visiting a pub nor having the brewery wagon delivering at their homes. It was perfectly in order for the Worthington to be delivered openly to the shop, since Father had the excuse that he had to oblige his customers, but the names of the customers would have come as a shock to many people had they ever been divulged. They never were, of course, and when I made my deliveries I referred to them as 'Blackbirds' and as the bottles were always covered with a white cloth and other groceries placed on top my mission looked completely innocent.

On Saturdays I was sent to collect order lists from those customers who were either too indolent or too housebound to bring them to the shop and when I had accomplished this task successfully for a few weeks Father got the idea that I might just as well try debt-collecting from debtors whose homes I passed on my way. At first I dreaded the thought, but after a little experience I came to enjoy it. There were so many intriguing characters among the 'bad payers' who greeted me with impenitent smiles and made such varied and colourful excuses for not giving me something off the bill that Saturday morning became the most amusing interlude in my week.

There was Mrs Howell who used to keep me standing at the door of her council house while she scrutinised the activities of her neighbours and talked to me of her sister who had done well for herself being housemaid at the home of a lord and lady. She rarely gave me anything off the bill but often after insisting that she 'hadn't a penny to bless herself with' she'd bid me wait while she ran upstairs and returning with some trinket which she'd bought from the market the evening before she would bestow it on me, assuring me that it was a valuable gift originally given by the lord and lady to her sister. She appeared convinced that the gifts reduced her outstanding debt, though needless to say Father was not of the same opinion. Mrs Howell had a son about twice my age of whom she was very proud and if he was at home when I called she urged him to come and show me whatever he had bought new during the week. 'Come and show the Miss your new cap, Amos!' she'd yell, and Amos, grinning all over his shiny red face, would come shambling obediently to the door and I was expected to express admiration. Once it was a new racing pigeon, another time it was a pair of fancy sleeve bands for keeping up the sleeves of his shirt and once to my consternation she called, 'Come and show the Miss your new false teeth, Amos!' and he came grinning gummily with the teeth proudly displayed on the palm of his hand. I didn't call there for three weeks after that.

Only a few doors away from Mrs Howell lived Mrs Spice, a tall bony woman with watery eyes and a voice as thin as a thread, who regularly gave me sixpence off her bill simply, I suspected, to encourage my calls. After ushering me into her living room as if I was an important caller she left me while she went to get her purse, giving me the opportunity to scan the lurid novelette which lay on the sofa. Every time I called on Mrs Spice there was a different novelette lying on her sofa as if just discarded, and once, catching me reading avidly, she had blushingly confided that she and Mr Spice loved to read the stories to each other in the evenings, taking the parts of the hero and heroine and acting all the romantic love scenes. 'We feel just like Pearl White and John Gilbert,' she told me, and I had to make an excuse to leave hastily because I felt myself erupting with laughter at the idea of large Mrs Spice and comic little Mr Spice kissing and embracing on the sofa and imagining themselves resembling glamorous film stars.

Mrs Balmy lived in a different part of the town and her reception of me was unpredictable. Sometimes she would open the door a crack and snap 'Not this week', yet at other times she would invite me into her kitchen and offer me a cup of tea which usually resulted in my listening sympathetically to her tirade against her husband, who, she claimed, was supporting another woman, and eventually being rewarded with a shilling off the account.

I was invited into Mrs Balmy's kitchen one day and saw that it was looking very bare.

'Are you wondering what's happened to the dresser?' she asked.

'I noticed it had gone,' I admitted.

'I've sold it,' she explained. 'And one of the easy chairs.' She gave me a look of defiance. 'And I'm going to sell a lot more before I'm finished.' She dived into a cupboard beside the fireplace, brought out a man's tattered slipper and thrust her hand into the toe. 'That's some of the money I got for them,' she told me, unclasping her hand to reveal two pound notes and some silver. 'And that money's mine and mine alone. I'm not letting that blackguard of a husband get it from me.' Her voice had grown shrill, but it softened as she went on speaking. 'I wouldn't have had the guts to do it, though, if it hadn't been for my father. He's been wonderful to me. Only last week I was sitting on that chair you're sitting on and I was breaking my heart crying when suddenly Father comes in. He put his hand on my shoulder. "Don't cry, Nell," he said. "Just plan ahead and make things comfortable for yourself." It was my father that told me about my husband's tart. It was him that told me to sell the furniture and keep the money in a safe place ready for when my husband leaves me. He says he knows for sure he will leave me.'

She put back the money and pushed the slipper into the cupboard. 'He's a wonderful man, my father, but I don't suppose you ever knew him.'

I had been listening to her with awe. The only thing I knew about her father was that he had been dead for at least three years and, disconcerted by her speaking of him in the present tense, I stood up thinking I would ask for something off the account and then get out quickly. I was just opening my mouth to speak when she hissed a command. I stared at her. Her eyes, always over-bright, had grown rapturous and she stood up, slowly raising her hands as if she was trying to catch a balloon.

'He's coming!' she announced.

I made ready for a hasty exit. I had heard enough about life in that district to appreciate how violently a husband might react if he came home and found his wife had in his absence sold a good deal of the furniture. To my relief I could neither see nor hear any footsteps approaching. I attempted to speak again but again Mrs Balmy gestured me to silence.

'He's coming!' she repeated. 'I know he's coming.'

'I can't hear anyone,' I said.

Mrs Balmy clutched my arm. 'Be quiet!' she whispered. 'You might drive him away.'

'Who?' I asked, bewildered.

Her reply made my body clench with terror. 'Father!' she exclaimed. 'He's in this room now. Can't you feel how the room has come alive? Can't you smell that wonderful scent? Father always puts scent on when he comes to see me so that I won't be put off by the grave smell, don't you, Father?' She gave my arm a little impatient shake. 'Smell!' she ordered. 'Take a long deep breath and sniff.'

I took a short panting breath but could only distinguish the smell of onions which were strong on her own breath. I tried to wriggle free of her arm while I still had strength in my legs to escape. She only held me closer.

'Father.' She spoke softly. 'Father. You don't mind this young lady, do you? She's come to ask for something off the bill I couldn't pay. Shall I give her something this week or will it be best to leave it till another time?'

She paused as if listening and then nodded to me. 'Yes, he says I can give you a shilling this week. There's my purse on top of the gramophone; take the money and leave the receipt.' She let go her hold on my arm and turned away. Trembling, I extracted a shilling from the purse and, desperate to get away, threw over my shoulder the suggestion that I should give her the receipt next week.

'Oh, no,' said Mrs Balmy. 'Father says you must leave the receipt now, don't you, Father?' She lifted up her arms as if resting them on someone's shoulders and while I wrote with shaking fingers I distinctly heard the sound of a kiss. I tore out the receipt and was halfway to the door when Mrs Balmy called me back.

'Put the gramophone on for us, love,' she entreated. 'Father wants me to dance with him.' Except for brief glances in my direction she was looking adoringly at a space about two feet in front of her. 'What's it to be this time, Father? A waltz? I knew it would be. Your favourite?' She indicated the door of the cabinet. 'Put on the "Blue Danube", love. That's his favourite. But you'll have to put a new needle in.'

Too scared to disobey I was glad to see there were only three records in the cabinet so that the 'Blue Danube' was not difficult to find. I was sweating as I fumbled with the new needle, placed the record on the turntable and wound the handle only just enough for the turntable to gain speed before I lowered the arm. The scratchy strains of the 'Blue Danube' filled the kitchen as I made a dash for the back door, but even before I was safely outside the gramophone had started to run down. As I passed the window I glanced fearfully into the kitchen where an ecstatic Mrs Balmy, appearing oblivious of my exit and of the languishing music, continued to waltz around the kitchen as if held in someone's arms. It was my last glimpse of Mrs Balmy, for when I told Father of my experience he said I mustn't go there again.

Two of our most difficult debtors were Mrs Quaver and Mrs Brady. Mrs Quaver owed a large bill which, despite my regular calls, she made little attempt to pay off until eventually Father went to see her. When he returned I was told I was to have piano lessons. We had recently inherited Grandfather's handsome rosewood piano which with its red pleated silk panel and brass candleholders now had pride of place in our sitting room. I longed to be able to play it, so that when Father disclosed that Mrs Quaver, before her marriage, had been a piano tutor and had offered to pay off her bill by giving me lessons I was enchanted. With my new music case in which was a *Smallwood's Tutor* I set off at a quarter to nine the following Saturday morning and presented myself at Mrs Quaver's, who accepted with equanimity my change of role from debt-collector to pupil. She bade me sit on the double piano stool and placed herself beside me and immediately I wished I could go back to my former role.

Mrs Quaver smelled so abominably that I much preferred to meet her at her front door than to share a piano stool with her for an hour.

Mrs Brady had no accomplishments. She was a sharp-featured woman with hostile blue eyes who seemed to regard running up debts in the town as a pastime from the consequences of which she was protected by the fearsome reputation of her husband. I hated going there since more often than not I was greeted by a shrill reprimand for daring to ask for money coupled with a threat to 'tell my husband'. It was sheer stubbornness that made me continue calling on Mrs Brady, Father having told me that I could leave her to him, and he had insisted that if I did call I must make sure it was before twelve o'clock so that there should be no chance of Mr Brady being at home. Mr Brady was a big strong Irishman with a big strong Irish temper, and his neighbours, even his drinking cronies, went in terror of him. His attitude to everyone was one of sneering contempt and his Saturday fights outside the pub were notorious. It was said that on one occasion when a man standing at the bar had made a mild objection to something Brady had said, Brady had seized his hand and grasping the thumb had pulled it right off. Mrs Brady, shrewish as she was, was equally fearful of her husband, but her brazen manner prevented people showing her the slightest sympathy. Mrs Brady grew increasingly cheeky about her debt until at last Father went to visit her. He was no more successful than I and so angry was he that I heard him telling Mother he proposed to call when Brady himself was at home and tackle him.

I was terrified, imagining what Brady might do to Father, and the next time I went debt-collecting I deliberately waited until after twelve o'clock before I called on the Bradys. The big Irishman was working in his patch of front garden staking sweet peas which were the only flowers he allowed to grow. Gathering all my courage I opened the gate and went inside. Mrs Brady, opening the back door, gestured furiously at me to go, but I stood my ground. Brady looked up, assessed me and turned away. My knees were quivering.

'I've come for something off the bill,' I managed to say.

Brady straightened up and took three slow strides towards me. I was ready to run, but I stared up at his coarse red face towering over me, telling myself that I could dodge swiftly and that he wouldn't dare touch me.

'What bill?' he demanded truculently.

'The bill Mrs Brady's been owing for nearly two years,' I replied.

He fixed me with a furious stare, but I wouldn't look away. 'You cheeky young bugger,' he muttered.

'She hasn't paid anything off it for months,' I added.

'How much is it?'

I knew the amount off by heart, but I opened my book. 'One pound and sixpence,' I said.

Brady grunted something I could not hear and turning went into the house. I heard a great bawl followed by the sound of footsteps running up and then down the linoleum-covered stairs and I moved nearer the gate thinking Mrs Brady might have been sent to get some means of chastising me. Brady, his expression even more furious, came out again holding a pound note in his hand.

'Take this,' he said, 'and don't come back again.'

I took the pound note. 'And sixpence,' I said, timidly, knowing I wouldn't get it.

'That's all you're getting,' said Brady, watching me. I was trembling so much that I dropped the note when I was putting it into my purse.

'Don't you want it?' Brady's voice sounded fierce, but looking up I saw what looked like a small shy smile playing round his mouth and suddenly I knew I need not be afraid.

I had the gate open before I said, 'You still owe me sixpence.'

'Wait a minute, then,' said Brady. He put his hand into his pocket and I thought with astonishment that he was going to give me the sixpence, but instead he produced a pair of secateurs. With them he snipped off a bunch of sweet peas.

'Here you are,' he said. 'There's sixpennyworth of sweet peas. That means I'm owing you nothing, so keep away from here in future.'

Father looked cross when I told him I'd found Mr Brady at home, but his eyes opened wide when I showed him the result and his displeasure changed to admiration.

'By Jove, Chipcart,' he said, 'you've given me the surprise of my life.' He turned to Mother. 'What do you think of that?' he asked her.

Mother looked disdainfully at the bunch of sweet peas. 'There's not sixpennyworth there,' she said.

There was one household where, though they owed money at the shop, I called at not to collect the debt but to take a rice pudding or a bowl of meaty broth. It was a tiny little house opening direct on to a narrow alleyway and it seemed that the only living room was too small and too dark for the front door ever to be shut. The place was crammed with old furniture; coats hung on the walls; a baby lay in a banana-crate cradle, while other children crawled or toddled over the newspapers which were intended to protect the newly washed floor. The tablecloth, too, was newspaper and usually when I called the only food on it was a jar of jam with a knife stuck in it and half a hacked-at loaf. When I proffered the thick, cold rice pudding the dish was always put on the floor and the children grabbed fistfuls, squeezing the gluey pudding into their mouths and dropping lumps which they retrieved from the newspapers after the dish was emptied. I could never understand why my parents thought the family worthy of their benevolence since I sensed that I and the food I brought were resented. Ebby, the husband, who repudiated all work, used to glare at me from his chair beside the fire with aggressive black eyes that had the sticky shine of cheap varnish, while Mart, his wife, drab and shapeless as a bolt of black cloth, sat opposite him, hands fidgeting in her lap and apprehension all over her long yellow face that always made me think of a bar of scrubbing soap left for too long in water.

No one ever greeted Ebby with 'Are you working?', they were too afraid of a burst of abuse. The only time he was known to have applied for work was when one of the horses belonging to the local timber merchants fell ill and the vet ordered that he must be given a bucket of beer at two-hourly intervals all through the night. The timber merchant let it be known he needed men to sit up with the horse and though every drunkard in the town flocked to volunteer Ebby was in the lead. The horse recovered quickly but people said Ebby took a long time to recover from his lack of sleep.

'Why do I have to take food there?' I complained fretfully when I saw Mother putting yet another rice pudding into a basket and covering it with a cloth. 'Ebby looked so angry last time I thought he was going to order me out of the house.'

'But he let the children eat the pudding,' she countered.

I told her how they had eaten it. 'It's horrible having to watch them,' I said.

'Poor Mart,' Mother observed.

'Why poor?' I demanded.

'Because she's married to no-good Ebby.'

'Why did she marry him?'

'Because she did.' Mother was growing impatient.

'Couldn't she marry anybody else?' I persisted.

'Mart could have married plenty of men. She was a beautiful girl when she was young and always happy and laughing. She was going to marry a fine young man, but one day someone came along and told her he had another woman in Chester. It wasn't true. He had a brother who was courting in Chester but Mart didn't wait to find out the truth. She ran off and married Ebby and when the young man found out he killed himself.'

'Poor young man!' I ejaculated.

'Poor Mart,' said Mother again. 'Now just you be careful with that rice pudding.'

I wished my parents could have been as sympathetic to Mrs Bone as they were to Mart and Ebby. Mrs Bone was the wife of the manager of the gasworks and I remembered when she had first become a customer at the shop. She had been welcome then and treated almost like one of the gentry by my parents, but suddenly there was a scandal; a police-court case, and Mr Bone was sentenced to a term of imprisonment. His offence concerned the disposal of gasworks coal or coke and involved several of the town's most influential people, but though I heard Father declare his belief that Mr Bone had been made a scapegoat in the affair he behaved harshly to Mrs Bone when, with her husband in prison and herself and her family ejected from their lovely home, she came to Father and told him there was no prospect of her being able to pay her bill at the end of the quarter. Father refused to believe she had no money and despite her pleadings would not allow her any further credit. Mrs Bone's name was added to the list of debtors on whom I had to call every Saturday and never did I visit a house with such reluctance; Mrs Bone was a broken woman. Young as I was I could see that and I suspected that she was often cold and hungry. The small council house she now rented rarely boasted a fire and I once found her opening out packets of tea in case there should be any stray leaves hiding in the folds of paper, yet, if there was money in her purse, when I called she gave me something off her bill. Often I left Mrs Bone weeks at a time without calling on her, telling Father either that she was out or had no money and when I resumed my calls I could see how much frailer she was and how slow her movements had become since my last visit. After one such spell of missed calls Father thought Mrs Bone was not trying hard enough to pay off her bill and subsequent to an unpleasant interview with the bank manager about his own overdraft he called on her to see if he could extract money from her. He came back and with grim satisfaction showed Mother an insurance policy Mrs Bone had given him as security. It was for fifty pounds and though her debt was for only twenty pounds the policy was not due for repayment for another three years when, they had both agreed, she would take thirty pounds and give Father the twenty owing to him. I was thankful my constant badgering of Mrs Bone could cease at last, but though I did not call at her house I sometimes saw her groping her way about the garden, for now she was going blind, and with some thought of helping her I added her name to the list of people I prayed for each night.

The day the insurance policy came up for repayment Father left soon after breakfast to visit Mrs Bone and within an hour he was back.

'You've really got it at last?' Mother's voice was a mixture of hope and fear.

'Yes, there it is. Four five-pound notes.' Father slid them out of the envelope and put them one at a time on the counter. 'One, two, three, four . . .'

I watched miserably, thinking of poor blind Mrs Bone and hating the shop because it seemed to me it had made Father greedy for money.

'You shouldn't take it,' I said. 'She's so poor.'

'She wouldn't be poor if her husband hadn't done wrong,' retorted Father sternly.

'But she couldn't help it,' I argued.

'You be quiet! You don't know what you're talking about,' Father snapped. 'D'you think we keep a shop to give stuff away?'

I slipped away up to my bedroom where I lay on my bed pondering dramatically impractical ways of helping poor

Mrs Bone and vowing that if I could somehow amass some money I would immediately hand it to her. The opportunity came less than six months later. One of the houses where I collected orders on Saturday was the home of an amateur racing tipster and so frequently did his wife mention having 'picked up a bit from the gee-gees' that I started taking the tips she passed on and putting a sixpence or even a shilling of my pocket money along with the name of the chosen horse into an envelope that the errand boy secretly collected and dropped through the curate's letter-box on the evening before a race. Since some of our most exalted customers placed bets and the curate was not averse to acting as a 'bookie's runner' my parents could see nothing wrong with my having a little flutter, particularly since the tips I got were usually good ones. Rarely was my stake more than sixpence or my winnings more than ten shillings, but one day the tipster's wife suggested I back what she called a 'treble'. I took her advice and when my winnings came there was over five pounds. So much money was intoxicating and I rubbed the lovely notes between my fingers. Mother's eyes glowed too at the sight of my winnings.

'I'll take you to Liverpool on Monday and you can buy yourself a new outfit,' she promised.

'Will you, honestly?' I breathed, and immediately started to plan my new clothes.

It was not until the name of Mrs Bone automatically slipped into my prayers that night that I remembered with dismay my vow to help her. The remainder of my prayers degenerated into a defensive argument with the Almighty. I got up and going over to the dressing-table lifted the lid of the box where I kept the money. I fingered the notes and thought of my new outfit and realised that I had no intention of keeping to my vow. I got into bed, knowing that when it came to parting with five pounds I was a true daughter of my parents.

15

As I grew older and school and homework took an increasing amount of my time, so, correspondingly, the shop seemed to increase its demands on my parents until home life dwindled into rushed meals and snapped orders. Although I had the near physical presence of my parents I resented the lack of opportunities for communication with them while they on their part, fearing their absorption in the business might result in too much freedom for me when I was at a dangerous age, imposed restrictions on my leisure which made it difficult for me to have friends because so often I was debarred from sharing in their activities. I had no Fran to confide in now since her mother had died tragically and she and her father had emigrated to Canada. I was lonely. I grew to hate the shop, blaming it for the change in my parents and for the disruption of family life and the less I had to do with it the more relieved I was.

Mother, who had repeatedly tried employing girl school-leavers to do the housework, found they were unsatisfactory unless under constant supervision and had grouchily resorted to coping with it herself which resulted in her flaring temper threatening to upset not only me and Father but also the customers. Both my parents realised they were working under great strain and I think they were at their wit's end devising ways and means of overcoming their difficulties when suddenly Letty came into our lives.

Letty, a remote relative of Uncle Dick's, had been orphaned as a small child and fostered along with her elder brother and sister by a harsh overbearing couple who gave a home to the children only for the work they expected to get out of them. The brother had become a coal-miner and by marrying had escaped his serfdom. The sister had been 'rescued' by the fractionally less overbearing Aunty Rye and had later married and settled down, but Letty, the youngest child, had stayed until while still in her early teens she had one day been raped by a stranger passing through the village. Despite doses of every known concoction to inhibit pregnancy she had given birth to a baby girl who had died within a few hours, and Letty, now repudiated by everyone she knew, had been banished to work in a remote farmhouse where it was intended she should be concealed and forgotten. Forgotten she was until her sister died suddenly of a stroke, and her brother, on hearing the news, felt it his duty to seek out his younger sister and if possible bring her to the funeral. He found her well fed but clothed in rags, her original employer having died and left her to the care of two eccentric old brothers who had never paid her a penny in wages nor bought her a stitch of clothing. Her brother, conscience-stricken at having neglected her for so long, bought and borrowed black clothes and for the first time in years Letty came out of her seclusion as bewildered as a castaway returning to civilisation.

It was at the funeral that Father met her brother and heard Letty's story. When he came home he talked with Mother for a while, Letty was invited to tea and the result was that she was offered a home and a job with us. The following week I went with Father to collect her and her tiny parcel of belongings from her brother's house and bring her home. She proved to be a dear person, illiterate but phenomenally hardworking, cheerful, kind and generous, with a childish appreciation of the new clothes, sweet cakes and gaudy trinkets she was now able to buy for herself. From the moment she settled in with us life became more tolerable.

With Letty taking charge of the housework and much of the cooking Father reckoned Mother would have more time to devote to the business and as sugar was now coming in cartons which saved a good deal of weighing up and salt was coming in packets so that it had no longer to be dug from a large block, he decided the time had come to extend the shop. Trade was flourishing; a big new paper mill had been built in the district bringing an influx of workers including strange people called 'Londoners' who asked in strange accents for strange foods like 'cornflakes' and 'boudoir biscuits' and brands of tea we had never heard of, which meant he had to keep a more comprehensive selection of goods. By demolishing the wall which had divided it from the old kitchen the shop now became almost twice its original size. He next bought a bacon slicing machine and persuaded ninety per cent of the customers that machine-sliced bacon was just as good and more economical than hand-sliced, but there remained the die-hards, and these included himself, who continued to insist on their bacon being hand-sliced, maintaining that machine-sliced bacon lost much of its flavour in the process.

Round about this time a grocer in the dockland area of the town went bankrupt and since he was a friend of Father's he offered us his remaining stock and fittings. Father hired a lorry and he and I along with the errand boy went to sort through and select from the accumulation of years in business those items which would be of most use to us. We found large old-fashioned metal canisters, painted in green and gold with exotic pictures of natives at work picking coffee and tea, planting rice, scraping sago palms and doing other tasks which we could not identify, though each picture was intended as an indication of the contents of the canister. There were hundreds of unused black wallets for which I could deduce no purpose.

'What are these?' I asked Father.

He took one from me, handling it as if it was some long-forgotten love letter. 'You're too young to remember these,' he explained, 'but in the time of the Great War we used to have ration books for food and these were the wallets to keep them in.' He handed it back to me. 'They're no use to us. You may as well throw them out for burning.'

We found a coffee mill with a large brass funnel and a handle nearly as big as that of a mangle.

'We'll find a use for that,' said Father. 'I guarantee even you will get to like coffee once you've smelled the beans being freshly ground.' We ferreted around and eventually found a small bag of beans. Father tipped some into the brass funnel, turned the handle and the deserted, sour-smelling old shop was filled with the aroma of fresh coffee.

He smacked his lips, winked at me and carried the mill out to the lorry.

Last of all we found three half-hundredweight sealed canisters. They were unlabelled and as we had no tool with which to prise them open Father loaded them on to the lorry. Mother and I stood over him as he got a chisel under a lid and forced it open. The tins were full of small white tablets.

'What on earth can they be?' asked Mother.

'I think I can guess,' replied Father, and popped one into his mouth. He nodded affirmatively. 'Saccharine tablets, left over from the war. Fancy the old joker hanging on to those for the last ten years.'

'What I would have given for those during the war,' moaned Mother.

'Aye, and they're as good and fresh as new.' Father hammered back the lid. 'There's no use for them now, though. There'll never be another war in our time so we may as well get rid of them.' The next morning he got up at six o'clock, loaded the tins on to a handcart and took them down to the canal where against all regulations he dumped them.

The following winter Father suffered a bad attack of rheumatism which confined him to bed for two or three weeks. Mother carried on heroically in the shop while Father, propped up with pillows, still managed to do the ledger work and bills. For years he had contributed to a sick club without ever having drawn any payment and now that he was incapacitated he resolved to apply for benefit. The clubman, who seemed to resent a man in Father's position receiving compensation, had to be taken into the sickroom to ascertain that Father was actually bedridden before he grudgingly countenanced the first payment. He could quite easily have come upon Father at his book-keeping had it not been for the fact that the clubman wore boots that squeaked his progress up the stairs and along the landing, giving Father time to push the ledger and papers under the bed and lean back wanly in time to receive him. This small deception was a continual source of amusement to Father and little did 'Mr Squeak', as we dubbed him, realise that his visits had a certain therapeutic value.

Although he recovered from his illness and resumed working as hard as ever Father suffered continually from backache and eventually the doctor diagnosed kidney trouble. He grew frailer. A specialist was called in but could give us no hope.

On the day of the funeral among the customers who came to offer condolence and tributes was dear old 'Irish', offering a bunch of flowers while great tears flowed down her anguished face, and Mrs Dainty, sobbing into the collar of her coat as she handed in a wreath. The errand boys hovered around with red-rimmed eyes and stricken expressions and Mr Josh came up to me and wheezed, 'He was a nice bloke, your dad.'

Mother struggled on, keeping the shop going with the help of an assistant, but without Father's flair and enthusiasm it became for her nothing more than drudgery. I had already embarked on a career of my own and was able to look after myself, so the business was sold. Mother retired with Letty to the 'cottage in the country' which Father and she had dreamed and talked of so much in the last two or three years before his death.

I have little to remind me now of the shop: only a knack, acquired during years of practice at 'weighing up', of being able to guess quantities to within a quarter of an ounce; four volumes of *The Practical Grocer*; the old cheese-tasting knife and the little brown barrel that for so long stood on the mantelpiece and was known as 'The tomtit on the round of beef'.